SILTON SEASONS

From the Diary of a Countryman

R.D.Symons '65.

SILTON SEASONS
From the Diary of a Countryman

R. D. SYMONS

Doubleday Canada Limited, Toronto, Ontario
Doubleday & Company, Inc., Garden City, New York
1975

To Hope
at Meadowlark Cottage in Silton.
With my love.

Library of Congress Cataloging in Publication Data
Symons, R D 1898–1973.
Silton seasons.
Bibliography: p. 195
1. Country life—Saskatchewan—Silton. 2. Silton,
Sask. 3. Symons, R. D., 1898–1973. I. Title.
S522.C36S95 1974   917.124'4 [B]
ISBN 0-385-07529-4
Library of Congress Catalog Card Number 74–2724

PREFACE

The man who sits to rest for a moment on the beam of his plough and looks at the earth and picks up a handful of soil and wonders about the mystery of life, recognizes that there is in that little handful something near to God himself. He unconsciously—although not in a highly educated sense—becomes a man of great wisdom. I am prompted to ask the question "Who is greatest among us?"

By kind permission of the Hon. Walter R. Shaw,
former Premier of Prince Edward Island
(*from a speech made to a convention on education*)

I am a countryman, descended from many centuries of Cornish countrymen. All my life has been spent in the country, at country pursuits.

This does not mean I have been a stranger to the urban scene. London, Paris, New York, Montreal, Ottawa, the prairie cities, and the lovely young cities of Canada's west coast—I know them all. But the urban fare is too rich as well as too hectic for me. Just as a bronco horse will leave the box of oats after a few mouthfuls and return to munching the dry, crisp prairie hay, so do I sicken after a week—or two at most—and return thankfully to what I know to be my natural environment.

I had my choice. Nobody and no circumstance forced me.

My boyhood was spent in a secluded Sussex village, where rooks gathered in the elms at dusk, and lapwings lamented by day over the ploughland.

Since I was sixteen I have spent my life on the wind-swept ranchlands of Saskatchewan, in the solitudes of the northern forests, and on the vague northwestern frontiers of Alberta and British Columbia.

Electric lights, automobiles, inside plumbing, these things were never for me. My camps have been in the sagebrush, in the willows beside gleaming waterways, in the shelter of dark spruces. My houses have been of logs, my fuel the good dry wood, my meat what the woods and streams provided or what my corrals were able to yield.

It goes without saying that, although country life fitted me like a comfortable old garment, I have had my share of discomfort and hardship, of hunger and cold of the sort which might daunt many. Naturally I have suffered disappointment and defeat, and I have sinned and been sinned against; but these things lead to contrition and forgiveness, and therefore to growth.

And growth of the soul is the only real growing up. When first I started to edit these recordings about the prairies, an area just as interesting as the wilderness, if less romantic and exciting, my intention was to put the seemly and graceful world of nature, operating under its ancient and unchanging laws, in contrast with the urban life of rush and bustle and insensitivity and status symbols, and to take a very hard look at the modern welfare society and the technocratic state ruled by experts.

However, I finally decided not to emphasise what to many must be obvious, and instead have contented myself with trying to depict a rural scene which is fast changing, with only brief references to more disturbing thoughts. My advice to do this came from a very old source which says: "Leave off from wrath and let go displeasure; fret not thyself lest thou be moved to do evil."

My hope, therefore, is that the readers of these excerpts may draw their own conclusions where I have kept silent.

If my life has been spent with joy and beauty, it will be for you to decide whether it is my spirit or my pen which has faltered if I have not presented these observations worthily.

R. D. SYMONS

Silton, Saskatchewan
1965

Contents

EDITOR'S NOTE

R. D. Symons died on February 1, 1973, after a long and courageous fight against ill health. The news of his death brought sorrow to the legions of people who had known him in any of his many roles—as cowboy, soldier, game warden, rancher, lecturer, naturalist, artist, or fine neighbour and stout friend. But it was as a writer that he was able to reach the greatest number of people; even now, more than one year after his death, his publisher and his family still receive letters of admiration and gratitude from those who have come upon his books and fallen under his spell.

It is for these people that this book is being published. As can be seen from his Preface, Dr. Symons originally wrote *Silton Seasons* in 1965, when the flow of books that have since come from his pen had not yet begun. Nine years is a long time for a book to be fallow, especially a book that deliberately turns its attention towards the past and its contrast with the present. But while much of the book may be unfashionable in 1975, it can be argued that little of it is dated. For in the course of his wide-ranging account of the yearly cycle of country life on the prairies Bob Symons (he would approve of the informality) touches on the most important things in life, on Family and Love and Birth and Death and all the most important things of head and heart. And these things do not change and become dated.

Mrs. Hope Symons was pleased to hear of our plans to publish *Silton Seasons* because, in her words: "This book really *is* Bob."

For those who knew the man or have read his previous works, that recommendation will be enough; for those who have never before encountered his writing, a new friend speaks from the pages that follow.

D.G.

Toronto, 1974

"I consider it the best part of an education to have been born and brought up in the country."

A. B. ALCOTT

"If country life be healthful to the body, it is no less so to the mind."

RUFFINI

CHAPTER I

Escape to Silton

If you drive north from Regina, Saskatchewan, on highway No. 20, you will, shortly after crossing the Qu'Appelle Valley, see a gravel road leading to the west.

There is a signpost here which reads: "Silton 2 miles." All you can see to explain that sign is a quick glimpse of the top of a grain elevator, for this is a rolling, almost hilly country, dotted with bluffs and sloughs to tell you that you are in the parkland prairies.

Hope and I live up that road.

Our summer cottage is eight miles west of the village, overlooking the sixty-mile stretch of water called Last Mountain Lake. You might wonder at that name, for you see no mountain. But the map will show to the northeast an area called the Touchwood Hills. These used to be called mountains, and in a generally level plains country that was forgivable. The last outpost of these hills, separated from the main body by over twenty miles, lies about that distance north of Silton and perhaps twelve miles east of the lake. It dominates much of the landscape, even though it is only a low hill. The quite heavily wooded crest adds both deeper colour and a further illusion of height as you get your first view of it seven miles north of Silton. Early travellers from the East quite naturally called it the last mountain, for from its height they could look westward across the water to the vast expanse of translake prairies and see only a level horizon.

Silton, Saskatchewan, was named for Silton in the county of Dorsetshire, England, by Charles Benjafield, who came to the district in the early eighties. He died in 1912 and was buried in

the little cemetery just west of the village. This enclosed piece
of ground occupies the crest of a high hill overlooking the lake.

Silton is not a town, only a very small village. An old village
in terms of the settlement of our province, yet a very new and
callow one when we compare it to the wattle-house villages of
Celtic Britain, for less than a hundred years ago it was a buffalo
pasture under the hand of the red man.

The anthropologists like to tell us that man was once a wanderer,
migrating as the needs of game or water dictated.

The first step towards a more settled life—the taming of wild
sheep and cattle—was followed by a much greater one, the sowing
of seeds. Man saw, in the new art of agriculture, the possibility of
settling down in a chosen spot, and from this came the permanent
village.

Now, the man who excelled in making hoes or baskets, or in
tanning leather, could follow his chosen bent and live by trading
his artifacts for his farmer neighbour's grain.

Crafts and trade were born together, but back of both was always
the husbandman. This triple interdependence is still the basis of
our economy. In spite of centralisation, internationalised firms,
and changed concepts, many small communities exist as tiny worlds
within the greater—limited, it is true, in many ways and more
and more dependent on the larger centres.

But community ties, community activities, are still strong, and
this is what makes a village as opposed to a mere trade depot.

Village life was the beginning of civilisation; and it may constitute, someday, the last vestige—for we are in danger of losing
the arts which are civilising, by a blind adherence to "progress."

Village life dominated the ancient civilisations of the East.
Jesus was a village man. He spoke in the simple terms of village
language and thought. He told us of lost pennies, of barren fig
trees, of bushel measures, and of the flowers of the field which
put to shame the glory of kings.

The commercial jargon of every age dies out—as will the stilted,
soulless language of technology. Village speech remains.

"Father is late." "The hens are laying." "It looks like rain." We said these things in Chaldea, in Egypt, by the Ganges, on the Sussex downs, and on the shores of Nova Scotia. We shall be saying them when automobiles are obsolete and petroleum oil forgotten.

Silton village itself consists of one grain elevator, a store, a telephone exchange, a garage, and a post office—the latter being one room of a private house. These establishments, together with a number of dwelling houses, are scattered over perhaps eighty acres.

As we shall see, the village was once considerably larger, as evidenced by certain old foundations and by the groups of planted trees which originally sheltered these sites. Silton has not been immune from the shrinking effects which have left their marks all through the rural scene on these prairies.

The population does not exceed twenty families, of which nearly half are retired farmers whose children have grown up and left.

The surrounding countryside, which can be properly accredited to Silton by way of trade, comprises the area lying within seven to ten miles, but includes several small summer resorts on the lake. The rolling farmlands are occupied mainly with grain culture, but every farm has some cattle, and there are several good-sized herds of pure-bred Herefords and Angus of excellent quality.

Not much of the native grassland remains—perhaps 15 per cent —but what there is shows us how this land must have appeared to the first settlers. Throughout we see small bluffs or groves of white poplars, together with clumps of silvery wolf willows, saskatoons, and rose bushes.

Many other small towns and villages are within easy distance —Earl Grey and Southy to the east, Craven (in the Qu'Appelle Valley) to the south, and Strasbourg (a market town) twenty miles north in the shadow of Last Mountain.

There is nothing unique about Silton. It is no more than a tiny dot in the parkland prairies which stretch northwest to Edmonton and southeast into Manitoba, yet Silton represents a cross section of prairie life, prairie ways, and prairie people.

For all the shiny new cars and up-to-date machinery, it is still essentially rural, with a less rapid pulse than is seen in the cities and with a little more time to consider thoughts instead of being entirely preoccupied with things. The rural scene, too, with its natural environment, its animals, and its wider horizons, gives a little more understanding of fundamental principles of life and happiness in a day when facts are shot at us like bullets. We may see that it is better to understand the implications of one fact than to memorize a hundred.

Prairie and plains are not quite the same, in spite of the fact that geography books lump the whole of the interior country of North America under the term "Great Plains Region."

"The prairies"—from the French word for fields—was the descriptive name bestowed by the early explorers on the rolling, semi-treed savannahs into which they emerged from the hardwood forests of the Eastern States.

Originally, this term designated an open country of longish grass, set about with some trees and clumps of brush, with perhaps a pond or a hill in sight. The level grassland glades constituted the likeness of fields—so now "the prairies" is plural. One succeeds another. Some are very large, some small. Grande Prairie, Alberta, belongs to the former class, while Prairie River, Saskatchewan, is named for no more than a series of small meadows.

These parkland prairies, then, are not the treeless steppes stretching off to the south and west—the true Great Plains—nor the high plains of the Coteau, planted with short grass and sagebrush, the land of cattle roundups and the lean horsemen who ride in the alkali dust or turn their cheeks to the warm Chinook.

To the northeast in the Touchwood Hills, and to the southeast along the Qu'Appelle Valley, the native Crees still occupy the reserves granted to Pay-a-Pot, Pasqua, Poor Man, and other band leaders in 1875. Also, to the east, you can still see traces of the cart trail from Fort Qu'Appelle to the métis settlements of Batoche and Duck Lake on the south Saskatchewan—the

trail up which General Middleton led his troops in that sad
year of 1885.

The only railway then was the main east-west line of the Canadian Pacific, and there were few settlers and no village of Silton.

The Indians here were little impressed by the rifle shots on
the Saskatchewan, but quietly attended their traps and their gardens, so the site which was to be Silton never saw violence.[1]

From the eighties on, settlers came to take up the quarter-
section homesteads that had been marked out by the government
surveyors; came with creaking wagons drawn by slow, patient
oxen, making the twin wheel ruts in the prairie sod which
would link them to the main trails creeping snakelike from trading
post to trading post. We still see, sometimes, traces of these wilderness pathways, as we still see an old ox collar or a yoke hanging in some derelict shed.

The sons, the grandsons—even some great-grandsons—of these
pioneers are still around. Not all, by any means, for two wars
have thinned their ranks, and many more have married and moved
—but there is a representative smattering.

They are sturdy, handsome folk, these descendants of the
blue-eyed, ruddy-complexioned men and women who came from
England, Scotland, and Ireland across the seas or from the Mari-
times and old Ontario. They are cousins-german to the people
of Brandon and Plum Coulee and the Black Creek Stopping
House of Nellie McClung.

This locality never considered itself the "Wild West." These
early settlers had been reared in an atmosphere of orderly living,
nurtured in thrift and honesty and religion. They transplanted
their savoury herbs in their new gardens, and they fed them to
their young families. For they found these flowery fields, very
garden-like, where the shimmering poplars alternated with grassy
sloughs, where cool waters gleamed and rolling grasslands vibrated
with the songs of meadow larks and pipits. Here was rich soil
for the ploughshare, water for the stock, wood for the cookstoves,
stones for building, and limestone rocks to burn for mortar.

They built well, these people from Downpatrick, from Simcoe, from Peggy's Cove, from Lancashire, Dorset, Durham, and Kent; they built a new England, a new Ontario, under the Red Ensign which would forever insure that they were building Canada. Flavel, Swanston, Wright, Dale, Metcalf, Burrows, Robinson— these are just some of the names.

From here they sent their sons and grandsons to fight tyranny, their daughters and granddaughters to nurse the wounded, to drive trucks, and to build ships, in those desperate years when there was so little to cling to and we lived by faith.

From here young men and women have gone to positions of trust and responsibility far beyond the dim horizons guessed at by their forebears.

Times changed.

The branch-line railway came. Wagons gave way to cars. Horses, the so recent successors of the patient oxen, were discarded for tractors.

But, as Thoreau says, most inventions are simply another way of doing the same thing; and farming, trading, and raising a family do not change essentially. Fields must be cultivated, men must be fed, babies must be put to bed, and young people must fall in love.

Neither do the fields and groves change essentially, for the birds are still here. Even the buffalo birds, which Kelsey saw on the shaggy humps of the bison, have only changed their name. They are cowbirds now, and they perch on the humpless, swaying shoulders of the homeward-bound milk cows. The bright warblers still flash and twitter among the wild roses, and the flowers themselves still have the same fragrance which inspired many an Indian mother to name her baby daughter Sweet Prairie Rose.

The lake, in spite of the clusters of summer homes, still bears on her breast the handsome ducks and stately swans of yesterday, still holds within its depths the silvery whitefish and the savage, jewelled pike.

Meadowlark Cottage, our summer home, squats high on the bank overlooking the blue water of that lake at a spot called Pelican

Point. The first time we climbed that hill we were greeted by the fluting of one of these yellow-breasted birds, and the name came naturally to us. Nor has it proved a misnomer, for each spring a pair nests close by, and the male salutes us daily at sunrise.

From here, between the sparkling waters and the upland grain fields, I see a world untouched (except for the cottage area) by the plough; I see all I have just mentioned—the groves, the birds, the flowers. I smell the perfume of wolf willow in June, I hear the thrill of the vesper sparrow stealing across the greening grass of May.

But for the muffled sound of a far-off tractor, we might be—except at weekends—the first pioneers.

Here I wander, sketchbook in hand, in an earthly paradise, while Hope—more practical—bakes her brown bread and writes long letters to our daughter in England. Often she joins me, nonetheless, and when she sings the birds stop to listen.

Just as the métis buffalo hunters of long ago left the open prairies for the shelter of the Red River Valley, seeking the company of their kind at the approach of winter, so do we—Hope and I—move into Silton at that season, and once again become members of the village family till the April sun thaws the ice of Last Mountain Lake.

We are newcomers here. It was by the merest chance that we were offered a small cottage at Pelican Point and for the first time passed through the village of Silton. We added to and improved the building, for we wished to settle permanently. After many years spent in pioneering new settlements, in exploring the northland, and in ranching among the Peace River foothills, I wanted to see how fared the countryside I had known fifty years before—the older settlements of southern Saskatchewan.

We did not leave our ranch voluntarily, even then, but at the dictates of the doctor. Bitter it was to leave those lovely, remote rangelands with their mountains shining in the west. Sad it was to say goodbye to our horses, and realise we might never ride again. But we brought our saddles and our riding gear as mementos.

And it all turned out better than we had hoped. Here we have found leisure after many years of high endeavour. We have got to know every nook and cranny on the lake shore. We have wandered up the coulees and over the hills—and, above all, we have met the people, for we get our weekly groceries at Silton Store, which is a great meeting place.

The people, no less than the birds and the lake, have healed the wounds of parting from our Shangri-La, where the sturdy logs of our house muffled the howling of the timber wolves.

If an apology is required for offering these observations of a small world, may I suggest that the large world is made up of communities like this? And the life force of any community is found in the image of family life. Each such small ecological community, where man and beast and plant are all affected by rainfall, soil, and topography—no less than by inheritance, culture, and tradition—is a family of God, surviving cycle after cycle by virtue of the life force which activates it.

This is the pattern from which man stepped forth to occupy the earth. This is the underpainting of the canvas which is Canada. It is also, I believe, the underlying strength of this nation. We might well ask ourselves, as Canadians, has the weakening of these community ties and loyalties affected the ties and loyalties of our people as a whole? Is this why we must examine our Confederation anew? Was it the lack of a proper understanding of this which has divided urban and rural societies into two solitudes more real and more dangerous than those which divide French and English Canada?

Man's nature includes the animal. The process of development did not destroy the animal desires, but simply added free will above innocent instinctual motivation.

For too long this free will has been directed to the point not of contentment, but of power and wealth and so-called progress.

I may be criticized by some for mentioning such a thing as biological progress. To those who say this is an ungodly idea, I can only reply most humbly that in denying this very natural theory we put great limitations on the very Creator we say is omnipotent.

We are all dust of the earth—man and beast and tree. We come from dust and to dust we shall return, and to suggest that the Creator could take one kind of dust and not another to perfect his Creation in the image of man is hardly logical.

We need, I feel, to allow once more for this instinctual wisdom, which shows us values and beauty and good taste in living. Primitive man was not a fool, by any means. He knew better than to put all the eggs of the spirit in the basket of materialism. So in the following pages I may from time to time allow myself to look very hard at modern society, not with any wish to be unkind, but rather to show how, with our wealth, our power, and our pride, we have lost much which made life thoroughly satisfactory and full to our forebears in spite of their lack of modern conveniences; all for the very simple reason that man does not live by bread alone.

CHAPTER II

May—The Moon of New Leaves

Pelican Point forms the inner vertex of the acute angle formed by the lake, of which one arm extends ten miles east and the other about fifty miles north. The prairie level rises slightly, and pauses butte-like before rushing downward to the beach, and the actual point of sand and gravel thrusts itself several hundred yards into the lake, dividing the waters, so that an east wind will send breakers roaring in to fret and worry the sand on that side, while the west side will remain placid. When the wind blows from the north or west the process is reversed. The hundreds of gulls which occupy this sandspit in daylight hours know how to dispose themselves according to these winds. The few large rocks which dot the extremity are well whitewashed by these birds, which crowd onto them when threatened too closely by the spray.

I remember when the point was nearly half a mile long and adorned with clumps of Manitoba maple. In those days of forty years ago, the pelicans nested here. But today both trees and birds are gone, for the government dammed the outlet of the lake, raising the water level, and they were drowned out.

Today the last remnants of those shady groves are to be seen in the few waterlogged stumps which still lie among the weeds, but we still see pelicans on occasion, resting on the rocks or flying north from their fishing with purposeful beats of their great black-tipped wings. Sometimes they hold their wings still for a hundred yards as if wind-borne or wind-blown; but soon the beating recommences. So, beating and sailing in perfect rhythm, they become smaller and smaller and drift into the horizon, leaving us earthbound and in wonder at their aloof beauty.

The weed wrack at our feet is full of the broken remnants of those tiny lobsters we call crayfish. It is the gulls—and crows —which dart into the water and drag them out, and it is these birds which so cleverly dismember them for the tender meat. Most of these remnants are bleached white, but some are whole heads and claws with their little scissors, and these are bright blue, which is the colour they turn to in the first day or two. Fresh from the water they are pinkish, like shrimps.

Back from the sandy shoreline, the point is green with sweet clover, an alien plant escaped from the farmers, who grow it for fodder. Here in the sand it thrusts down its strong, long roots to probe the riches and moisture underneath; for in the old days this point was grassy and the topsoil was deep. Only since the damming has the shingle and sand been deposited there from either side according to the wind.

At evening, when the sun is near his setting, the gulls commence the northward flight to their roosting places in the reed swamps far away. Skimming in long lines just above the water, they pass between us and the low sun, interrupting the molten rays, so that the bright sky is seen as it were through a moving grill. The wake of the sun makes a golden pathway beneath the moving birds, a pathway which draws the eyes onwards to realms of unknown splendour.

The royal blue of the lake stops abruptly on either side of this sparkling track, and the water moves graciously from side to side, its surface undulating in all the dignity of a duchess's train.

These—the birds, the water, the wet, sandy tideline—are eternal, unchanging with the years. We lose all sense of time until we turn to the crooked shoreline which disappears to left and right behind us. There, below the humped outline of the overlooking hill, are the cottages of the city folk who weekend here and who each Sunday break the prairie silence and the peace of the waters with their power boats.

The little wooden buildings are disposed higgledy-piggledy about the rock slopes. The first line of transplanted suburbia touches on the beach. Later comers crowd behind, seeming to peer over the shoulders of those preferred ones for a glimpse of the blue waters.

After the glory that has been before our eyes, how futile, temporary, and drab these small buildings appear. It is as if they had inherited time and death from the hand of man, in spite of all attempts to conceal the inevitability of decay with paints of a hundred rainbow colours. There is something melancholy in this brash attempt to cheat in advance the forces which will soon overcome our attempts to take root.

Last Mountain Lake has changed little since the second ice age. The little wooden buildings have only been built within the last twenty-five years.

But over the first steep hill, on the upland, is a little hollow or amphitheatre, green with prairie grass and bright in spring with nodding clumps of wild onions. This is a farmer's pasture, because these undulating slopes of downland have not been thought worthy of the ploughshare's consideration. Few people come here, for this is the bald, rocky prairie which no cars can traverse, no motorboats navigate, and where no golf can be played. Within three hundred yards of the cottage, it is as remote as Tibet and as full of mystery.

In this hollow, then, I can show you something far more permanent, far more akin to the eternity of life, than the clustered settlements of wood and paint.[1]

If you will look closely as you approach, you will see little dimples in the herbage, and each of these will prove to be a stone, about which the grasses year by year build up the sod a little higher. And these stones, about the size of a man's head, are disposed in three large circles, averaging twenty feet in diameter. These are the circles where three airy Indian tipis once stood— how long ago one can only guess, perhaps forty years, perhaps a hundred.

The country people call these "Indian rings," and their purpose is obvious. These stones were placed round the tipis to hold down the edges of the buffalo hides which, sewn together, formed a covering for the framework of poles.

Was this a hunting or fishing party? Possibly, but I doubt it; for why was the camp not made in the proximity of water, on the lakeshore—perhaps in that grove of scrub maples?

Much more likely it was a scouting or small war party. In this hollow or fold in the hills, the tipis would be reasonably concealed; by taking a few steps west or east, the party could survey either of the long arms of the lake; and from a hundred yards to the north the approach of enemies from that direction could be observed. The clear field of fire of a quarter of a mile in any direction would be another asset, with a view unhampered by any lurking places such as coulees, bushes, or even large rocks.

It would presumably be the duty of someone in camp to make the long and tedious uphill climb with water; but even this was preferable to camping close to the lake in a situation which would lend itself to surprise attack.

I sit sometimes on a marbled and gilded limestone rock and look towards this old camping ground, with my thoughts out of time and date, and I think I can hear the thumping of hobbled horses—lean, fleet Indian mustangs. They crop the young grass, and pause and look intently now this way, now that, blowing softly, then they crop again—but their ears are not still, and flick back and forth, for they were foaled on these plains and know its hazards. Steadily they tear the squeaking grass, and their jaw muscles work back and forth over the bony structure below their liquid eyes.

Nor are their owners less alert. They sit at ease, seemingly, and the murmur of the Cree tongue is no louder than the rustle of the wind in the bent blue sage, but their hands and eyes are employed. Gear must be repaired, moccasins resewn, lances repointed.

From time to time a man rises with the grace of Apollo and stalks soft-footed and straight-toed to the higher ground, gazing long and intently into every patch of scrub, every coulee, every fold of the hills, till his eyes reach the blue distance.

I smile at my dreams. Are dreams perhaps fragments—spirits —of real events which happened long ago, and which continue to pass whispering around the world, to be received on rare occasions by the antennae of the spirit? Is that what imagination is? Are dreams, then, closer to truth than we think?

We know the red man dreamed and patterned his life around his visions. So dreamed these hunters of long ago, and passed noiselessly over the grasslands, now here, now gone; too wise to fetter themselves, as one tethers a horse, to possessions they could not keep, could not carry with them.

Wisdom is not learning. It is the gift of God, and it is intuitive, and to be trusted. It is truth, and all attempts to explain and rationalise do it to death.

What of the descendants of these campers? I think—and my mind rushes through the corridors of history seeking them. What? Are these poor helpless wards of the government, rotting on their reserves—are these really of the blood and bone of those mighty hunters of the buffalo, those eagles of the plains? What kinship, what bond, now exists between these flabby legs, these slack mouths, and the lean thighs and hawk eyes of the horsemen who held sway over a thousand miles of prairie grass?

They look to the settlements and the cities and see only hostility garnished with a pinch of pity. The representatives of a people who have sold their birthright for the shiny products of "a high standard of living" visit them at intervals—the blind leading the blinded.

The inner power, the will, the purpose of the Indian people lay not in books, not in isms, not in ideologies, not in possessions, but in tradition, in legend, in myth, in story. And over all was faith in the Great Spirit.

The white man destroyed this.

He sneered at their riches, for to his mind this was poverty. He ridiculed their stories. He misinterpreted their myths. He destroyed their Great Spirit. "Why trust in an abstract—has not man greater gifts?" they hinted, and they dangled before the red man's eyes the tinsel of cheap thinking, cheap goods, and that cheap substitute for wisdom which we call knowledge. They pelted him with facts. Work hard, they said, and you will be rich. Rich? In what? Gold, silver, land, possessions? What do you trade for these? Faith and happiness? Freedom? Wisdom? Understanding and values, and knowledge that the Great Spirit has gifts, that life is a prelude to death, that death of the body is not the end? Does not man continually trade happiness for pleasure? Animals are wiser, perhaps. The fox does not sell his den nor the bison his wallow.

The Indian of today drinks beer, drives a car, raises Cain on Saturday nights, and we say: "The Indians are coming around, soon they will integrate!" And those Lindas, Kays and Shirleys who meet the truck drivers with their beer on Railway Avenue— are they really kin to the Bird Feathers and Red Lilies, the soft, sweet, modest girls who in the long ago tended the cooking pots in the prairie dusk?

Perhaps their stories are not all dead. Perhaps a tiny flame still burns deep down under the shoddy cast-off clothing. Sometimes we think we see a reflection of this when they dance— clumsily—the old dances which were meant for moccasins and not for feet pinched into high-heeled shoes.

Perhaps they will keep, nourish, this spark.

To be laughed at is torture indeed. To be forgotten is worse; but perhaps after their slow martyrdom these red people will turn again in yearning and longing and pain to their story, the story that man lives only by the spirit—all else is death before the grave. Perhaps in time these people, revitalized, will try once again to show us—as they tried at the time of the treaties[2]— that knowledge is not wisdom, nor facts understanding; and then, perhaps, we shall dust off *our* wonderful Story and live again— our Story of the Cross, the Story of bravery and sacrifice and nobility of thought and purpose, which has been submerged in the power and might of man's inventions.

Once we, too, lived in the knowledge that to lose one's life is to find it; but now the bomb is more powerful than love. We desist from war from fear of our annihilation, not because we love our neighbour any more than of yore.

How long, I ask myself, shall we be made to bear the yoke imposed on us by those who love only abstractedly—who love only en masse and never individually? Science, Sociology, Anthropology, and Psychology—words; names; abstractions; ideologies.

These are not flesh, not blood, not birth, not life, and not death; not joy, sorrow, riches, or poverty; nor do they lead eventually to the vision of beauty which is somewhere beyond the horizon of man's mind.

I walk home in the dusk. Nights are cold at this time of year, and I think of the coffee Hope will have ready. I wonder as I walk, am I treading in the very footsteps of one of those men of long ago? Was it here—I pause, overlooking the receding shoreline—that he saw an enemy scout? Or did he, too, dream of another day, dream of how these rocks, this prickly cactus came here? Was it a whisper from here that reached the fertile mind of Henry Drummond as he sat by that eastern river and wrote:

De nort' win' know dem well, an' de prairie grass can tell
How offen it is trample by de ole tam botte sauvage.

I wonder, from my bed, do those hunters of long ago see me? Know me? As they tent in the Great Sandhills of Whapaki, do they peer from their dimension into mine and read my thoughts? Is it possible that their Great Medicine Man with his fan of eagle feathers can part the mist which separates us and say: "Here is a white man who might have understood; but it is late, it is too late."

Dreams!

In spite of the high power poles at Pelican Point we do not have electricity in our cottage, for somehow it would seem out of place.

Hope cooks on an old-fashioned wood stove, a fine sturdy thing which must have come West with some homesteader. It is a "good baker," as the savoury loaves will tell you as they lie belly up and steaming of a Wednesday noon. For Wednesday is baking day. On the ranch there were usually two bake days a week, but then the "creatures"—as Hope called the men—came in hungry to make inroads on the larder. She uses whole wheat and white flour mixed. I never see the brown flour but my mind goes back to the windmill on the hilltop of my natal village across the wide Atlantic —Udimore in Sussex.

But I am not a true South Saxon, for my blood like my name is Cornish, which is almost to say Welsh.

But the mill. There I used to foregather with Mr. Weston, the miller, whose head was powdered like any dandy's of the Regency. I used to watch him dressing the "French stones," which actually were imported, and of a lovely pink colour, as if touched with a Frenchwoman's rouge.

And here was born the inspiration which eventually drew me to Canada; for on the grain floor, among the sacks of pale Sussex corn, were bags lettered in boldest red: MANITOBA HARD WHEAT. Mr. Weston explained that he used this amber grain to mix with the native product. He had, he added, a nephew in Manitoba, at Portage la Prairie.

"Portage la Prairie!" How the words of that romantic place name tickled my young palate! I could hardly wait to get home to look at the atlas, repeating the words to my eager feet as the homing rooks tried to distract me with their caws.

Poplar-wood smoke has a delightful smell—a prairie smell— which reminds you of early bonfires. Today it is essentially the smell of the Peace River country, where poplar lands are being daily put to the plough. And this is the wood we burn now, as always in the past. We buy it, ready cut, from our farmer-cum-carpenter neighbour Bill.

Bill is of German extraction, from east of Silton, where many descendants of thrifty, efficient German settlers still live. He is a humourist who loves to have you believe that he is cheating you. He is also a man of great resource and bravery.

To get to the back of our cottage it is necessary to climb a very steep hill. Once, when Bill had brought me a load of gravel for this hill, something occurred which might have had a tragic ending. Bill had left his truck pointing upgrade with the emergency brake on. I didn't trust this mechanism and suggested to Bill that he remain in the cab and hold down the foot brake while I unloaded the gravel. But my pace was too slow for his fancy, and presently he, too, jumped from the seat, climbed into the box, and began to ply his shovel, directing me to stand on the road and spread.

All at once the truck began to move backwards. Bill jumped out. The truck left the grade. It was heading—or rather backing —straight for the neighbour's cottage below, where the family was sitting outside enjoying the cool of the evening. As they saw the danger coming they scattered. The truck gathered speed.

Bill—who is not a young man—gave two great giant strides, bounding down the slippery, cactus-strewn hillside in pursuit. One hind wheel struck a big rock, and as the vehicle momentarily paused the cab door swung open and Bill sprang inside. He spun the wheel sharply and the truck veered, missing the cottage.

One misstep, one mistake in timing, and Bill could have been caught as the door banged closed. He would have been badly hurt, perhaps dragged to his death, and the neighbour's flimsy cottage destroyed.

All Bill did was grin, roll a fresh cigarette, and drive the truck up the hill again. This time we blocked the wheel with a great stone.

Fellow cottagers from the city view our absence of electricity with a jaundiced eye. By what right—you could see the question in their raised eyebrows—by what right did this newcomer flaunt convention, refuse to accept the symbol of the new technocracy? Or, having always lived on the frontier, did he not know about these things?

If I was not aware of the existence of electric stoves, refrigerators, and washing machines, it was certainly their duty (and kindness) to inform me.

I was reproved many times, kindly and patiently. I was even shown catalogues. Did I not owe it to Hope? No, I explained. Hope was used to baking with wood, and washing by hand held no terrors for her; she would sing while doing it. I filled her tubs, fetched wood, and emptied the water. Besides, all my life I had risen to make my shavings and light the cookstove. I liked to do it. The home hearth is a sort of family altar, and who should be the priest but the head of the house? And I like to feel that first gush of warmth, to hear the crackling of the kindling, to smell the smoke, to see the smudge against the morning sky which tells you which way the wind is blowing and the degree of humidity.

Above all, there is the feeling of independence from centralisation and possible power failures.

To burn wood is also an acknowledgement to nature for her gift of the poplar tree.

Well, I was told, did I not realise that if I once got electric power I would find I couldn't be without it? I thought this a most excellent reason for not having it. I am already hopelessly tied to tobacco.

So convenient, they told me. Yet I find nothing inconvenient about striking a match on the seat of my pants and putting the flame to a coal-oil wick.

Of course, when you get power, they would say, your troubles will be over. They had not asked me if I *had* any troubles. In any case, I could hardly imagine that it would be as easy as all that. If Hope died . . . was I to switch all the lights on?

But I forgot. This is the day of problems. The most ordinary conversation will bring out, somewhere, the words: "Of course, your problem is . . ."

The "problem" might involve something as simple as whether you should go to bed or watch "Bonanza."

We like to speak of early springs and late springs. So often do we hear the neighbours say: "I never saw things so backward; why, the trees aren't even green!" Yet, from year to year, there is—curiously enough—only a few days' variation in the greening of the leaf. And this is irrespective of the local weather.

I have watched the poplar leaves open every year for half

a century, and for most of those years I have noted the date in a diary or journal. I can see from this that the average date for the first flush of emerald is May 12—that is, in this latitude. It is a day or two later in the Peace River country.

Mind you, I refer to the first *leaves*. Some time before that, the poplars put forth their catkins—their flowers—and these appear as a mist or veil on the bluffs, but it is not the light yellow-green of leaves. Rather it is more like a bluish-green wash, almost gray in certain lights. But it obscures the terminal twigs and looks dark against the sky, and is often confused with leaf opening. Otherwise, the apparent discrepancies in dates, on which people remark, can only be another manifestation of our natural tendency to forget the bad and remember only the good. As the White Queen said: "Jam tomorrow and jam yesterday—but never jam *today*." Last year was always perfect, and of course next year's crop will be a bumper! That is why we call this a "next year" country.

Certainly all bluffs do not leaf together. Certain groves will be well greened while others still stand naked. This must be due to the influence of different soils and locations on sap movement. Also, young trees open their leaves earlier than old ones.

Pastures, too, show a plain tinge of green now. They only await the first spring rains to become lush. The cattle are not quite settled yet, but wander from knoll to knoll cropping the young, sweet growth, for the hollows and north sides of hills are still brown.

Daily the herds increase as the new calves arrive. They are wobbly, big-kneed at first, but in surprisingly few days they are active and gambol like kittens.

The early crocuses have dropped their petals by mid-May—if not earlier—and, where the pale flowers once opened to the sky, you see little aureolas of what looks like copper thread on the now much elongated stalks. Seen against the sun these little halos have the misty charm of fairy blooms.

It is instructive to gaze at—to examine—these little things. It helps to orientate us. They are not to be despised or ignored.

Great things and great thoughts are made up of little things and their contemplation. A tiny spider gave renewed purpose to Robert the Bruce. Jesus did not think it unbecoming to speak of sparrows.

We perhaps lay too much stress on the gifts of man, which are not so wonderful after all. We simply put together the gifts of God and make a steam engine or a radio, and say: "Look what we made!"

We show too little respect towards the natural world; we are impatient and peevish in our contemplation, demanding that every-thing be changed frequently, like children reaching for new toys to suck the paint from.

If these gifts of men are so desirable, why our constant grum-bling, our discontent with them, our demands for more the minute we possess some? Is it that our mouths remember the acid taste of our first disobedience? Is that why we must trample on, shoot, kill, spray, poison, and destroy the Garden in revenge against that Tree of which the final bitter fruit is the Bomb?

If ideas propel civilisation, they can also destroy much which is civilising, and Joseph Conrad says: "Hang them!" Each, he says, takes a little of your substance; each carries away a crumb of your belief in a few simple notions which you must cling to if you want to live decently and die easily.

In place of the crocuses, it is now the turn of the three-flowered avens to unfold, and everywhere among the grasses we see their drooping, triple heads of wine red. The buffalo beans are not far behind; they grow from stout rootstocks and are yellow as spring butter.

The clumps of saskatoon are now in bloom, and the first leaves opening—not green yet, but rather purplish. Soon the choke-cherries—already leafed—will fill the air with the pungent, almost cloying odour of their lacy, creamy blossom heads. The banks of every coulee are overhung with them, promising a heavy crop of sour, black fruit.

Everywhere the white crowns of wild onions bend in the breeze.

These were much used as flavouring by the Indians, whose womenfolk dug them up with pointed sticks. The memory they bring to me is of their smell on the breath of workhorses newly caught up for the plough. All night the beasts had grazed, cropping the onion tops with the grass, and when bridling them you were very aware of this. Like the aromatic smell of wild mint in the slough hay we fed at noon, that wafted odour of onions is nostalgic to any ex-horseman.

The cackling of hens in every farmyard is another link with those older days. We remember how often our horses were frightened as we tied them in the barn and some old hen flew shrieking from the manger.

Not only the domestic but the wild birds are nesting now. We find the domed nurseries of meadow larks, and sometimes put up a mallard duck from the low, rough scrub, and search and find the pale olive eggs all heaped around with down, as a dish of curry is surrounded by rice.

Earlier, we had found that a pair of small falcons—merlins— had made use of an old magpie nest in plain view of our window. We now find the young are hatched, and our visit is greeted with a great to-do, the birds circling on sharply pointed wings, uttering their sharp *ke-ke-ke* in resentment. Curiously, we found a ruffed grouse brooding her eggs right below the same tree, among the dry, coppery leaves of last year. Her mate was drumming close by.

I have commonly noticed that birds of prey leave a circle of neutral, unhunted territory in the close vicinity of their nests or eyries—perhaps this is from an instinct similar to that among animals which has been called "the truce of the waterhole."

Some of the more northerly nesting birds—those which we see only as birds of passage—are still working their way towards the slowly warming tundra above the Arctic Circle. While most of the larger wild fowl—cranes, swans, and geese—are already arriving on those sodden and mist-shrouded breeding grounds, many of the shore birds are tardy, and we may still see black-bellied plovers standing on the dark ploughland, their heads turbaned in gleaming white; or at night hear their fluted *ter-LEE-oo* as they pass overhead, sure and confident of their ultimate destination.

Other passing shore birds—especially yellow legs—still haunt the sloughs. These are brimming full now, and the young grass is sending up green shoots at the edges, but unless we get copious rains fairly soon they will not carry enough water to float the ducklings which are even now in the egg, and their mothers will have to lead them down the hills to the lake itself.

Hundreds of ducks nest on the upland stubble field which is now being prepared for the new crop. Farmers always try to avoid destroying these nests. If they see them in time they wheel their implements to avoid them, leaving a small island of undisturbed stubble. Unfortunately, these patches are very conspicuous to the hungry, quartering crows, who too often swoop down to investigate. In many cases the result is as tragic as if the nest had been ploughed under.

In the larger marshes, the rails and coots call all night, uttering notes now discordant, now poignantly sweet, while all around the chorus of the frogs rises and falls, the peepers shrilling and the old bullfrogs coming in with a deep bass *ko-chunk*.

The red-necked grebe has a harsh, angry double or triple note, but the slender, swan-necked western grebes really charm us with their upward-inflected, twice repeated *kree-a-ree?* Usually these birds will be floating far out in the lake, and distance and water add a very particular charm to their calls on a spring night—one version of love's old, sweet song, unembarrassed, free, and joyful.

Fish are spawning. The pickerel have almost finished, and as we listen to the grebes we are aware that many of these spine-backed fish are still in the shallows; for they splash noisily, and sometimes the moon shows us a gleaming flank or back.

The pike have breasted the current of the small marshy creeks which flow into the lake at the north end. Steadily they have pursued their way; thick, pregnant females followed by eager, narrow males, in obedience to the command "increase and multiply." In the far shallows their journey ends, and they splash and thresh in the ecstasy of spawning. In the water they are coloured like dragons, bejewelled of eye, jawed and toothed like alligators, their long bodies changing colour from gold to black to dark jade green to mottled purple. Their spawn—masses of gilded orange balls the size of tapioca—might be, too, the seeds of dragons.

The spring haunts of pike are also the chosen breeding grounds of muskrats, whose domed homes we see in the deeper water, at the edges of the reed beds. Only lately the trappers were taking these little cousins of the beaver in the full prime of their glossy pelts, but now they are safe from man. Nevertheless, the parents must be on guard for their young—for the pike, once spawned out, will be hungry, and young muskrats are satisfying fare.

The world of four-footed animals is equally aware of the urgency of the season.

The striped gophers are carrying hay for their nests. Naturalists call them thirteen-striped *spermophiles* (or seed lovers), but to the country boy they are "striped gophers." One female gopher has found a way under our cottage. When it was built the front corners were laid on great rocks, for the ground is not level. The untouched prairie beneath still carries its original grass, but by now it is completely dead from lack of rain and sun. This grass is unbelievably soft and dry, and the little gopher has chosen it, rather than the now greening grass outside, for her nesting material. We saw her emerge from beneath the building, looking very whiskered—for her mouth was full of straws which stuck out a good four inches on either side. I have seen the little haymaker "mice" of the mountains (which are really conies) look the same way.

After a quick look she scuttled around the corner to the north. It is not easy to follow these lithe, grass-coloured creatures to the nesting hole. We saw her disappear into the little patch of snow-berry bordering the shallow ravine, and then lost sight of her. We thought her den was on the opposite slope.

But, lo and behold, she reappeared, empty mouthed, from the *south*. The ground slopes so steeply to the west that the bottom of the hill is out of sight. We now realise that her burrow must be there, and she had made an almost complete circle, burdened as she was, to deceive us.

Most of the neighbouring cottagers shoot these "pests," as they call them—for indeed they will nip the young peas and corn.

Each to his taste; but we would as soon lose a little green stuff as be without these charming and dainty creatures with their ochre and dark chestnut pattern. Perhaps if some of these "pests" were looked at more closely their beauty would be seen and appreciated, and their right to live—at least within bounds—recognised.

CHAPTER III

June—The Moon of Roses

We have birds on our windowsill. For many years I have painted birds and written about them; but mostly in relation to areas off the beaten track.

But these birds of ours are resort dwellers—I almost said suburbanites—for they are co-owners of our cottage property. They are not eagles or cranes or pelicans; they are not exotic inhabitants of mighty mountains or dry deserts—nothing so glamorous as that. But they are honest birds, home-loving birds, not ashamed to be known as common or garden ones.

As well as all sorts of visiting birds—tourists, as it were—there are six species which nest within sight of my study window. This window attracts a large number of insects, but the glass baffles them, and rather than being a nuisance to me they are my unwitting aids; for they attract the birds, which hop about on the windowsill and help themselves.

The sparrows, of course, are year-round residents, but of the five spring arrivals the robins are always first. There is something about robins that no other birds quite have. Is it perhaps their association with childhood stories—"The North Wind Doth Blow" and "The Babes in the Wood"? Or is it the calm and confident way they hop across the lawn—three hops and then an uptilted stance as if to say: "My garden looks well today!" And yet robins can be temperamental. Once they lose their nerve their fluffing and carrying on lets you know at once that danger is near.

At any rate, my robins forsook me this spring and built on the electric meter of a neighbour's cottage.

"You'll rue the day," I told them. "*I* am here all the time, but that apparently abandoned cottage will blossom at the weekend. People will come and they have a *cat*. You haven't seen it —but wait!"

But the robins paid no attention to me and nested on the site of their choice. The mother had laid three lovely blue eggs when Sunday brought the householders—and the cat! That did it. Cat got up to the nest. No, she didn't get a robin; but she tore the nest and it fell, breaking the eggs.

Next morning the robins moved back to my lot and began to build in their old quarters, an orange box tacked to the woodshed. Mother Robin had two more eggs to lay, and she was in a hurry. This second nest was a mere apology—a few wisps hurriedly knocked together, with none of the fine finishing and moulding that had been bestowed on the first solid and compact effort. But *that* had been built on an insecure foundation and, like many such edifices, it fell.

Within twenty-four hours the robins had an egg in the new home, and next day another, and Mother Robin settled down to the job of brooding the two.

In the meantime a pair of house sparrows had found a convenient ledge under the eaves, and soon began to gather bits of dry grass. But we had several days of high wind, and I observed that only about one in three of the straws reached the ledge, the rest being dropped in the current, so to speak. I cursed them for the litter, but patiently tidied it up.

Sparrows are a nuisance; they bother other birds and are too cocksure for my taste. They should be equipped with leather jackets and bicycle chains, and not try to pose as respectable citizens. However, I decided to leave these ones strictly alone; if they were allowed to nest in peace, I hoped they might possibly be content to live and let live. They probably would have—but for the eternal triangle.

An unmated cock sparrow arrived. He was a morose, peevish, and untidy urchin, and he chivvied the happily mated birds so unmercifully that they finally could stand no more. They turned on him and gave him such a clouting that he abandoned his attempt at forcing a divorce.

But he did not leave the premises. No; this irascible bachelor took up quarters beside my wren box, sitting all day on the perch outside and chirruping in his best whisky baritone in the hopes of attracting a nonaligned she. The fact that no sparrow could have kept house in the box did not deter him from his sparrow-in-the-manger procedure. The result was that, when my wrens returned from points south and started to unpack in their summer cottage, they were viciously assailed by the ragamuffin and put to rout.

I hunted up another old tin can and wired it up nearby in the hope that it would be considered a fair alternative by the wee birds. But I was a day too late.

To go back to the robins—a particularly bold crow, who was in the habit of sitting on a fencepost some sixty yards away, had spotted their activities. One morning before I was up I heard a *caw!* and then a thud on the roof right over my bed. In fear and trembling for my robins I jumped up. The robins fluffed. The crow cawed again, but when the screen door slammed behind me he departed.

I knew he would try again, and I couldn't watch that nest *all* the time, so I began to cudgel my brains. A scarecrow! Of course, that was the thing! I hunted up an old tweed jacket—it was one my wife had wanted to give to the Salvation Army but which I had saved by stealth. "Well, old vesture," I said when I found it, "here's a use for you." I draped it on a post near the nest and topped it with my third-best Stetson hat; one I'd bought in 1943.

Now, I am aware that Shakespeare warned us that we must not make a scarecrow and then let it keep its shape, till it becomes a perch, and not a terror; so I reminded myself that I must move its position daily. But when I went to do this, I discovered that the wrens had not been taught about scarecrows, and had started to fill one pocket with twigs and trash. This meant that I had to sacrifice still another garment. I chose for this a suit of recently discarded woolly intimates, for the weather was getting warm.

The wrens are very comfortable, and the bachelor sparrow, like all selfish creatures, is more morose and frustrated than ever. He does make occasional forays in the direction of the swallow box, which is another old apple-juice tin; but the spruce little tree swallows simply dodge him, and then when he looks around to see where they've gone they swoop up behind him so fast that his tail feathers are blown sideways and, like the coward he is, he makes off.

The swallows are the greatest lovers of the windowsill. They gorge themselves on fish flies within three feet of my writing desk and then sit preening their glossy, blue-black wings. The mother swallow is sitting now, and I see little of her. I watch her husband fill his beak and fly to the nest opening, and she puts out her white throat and tiny bill until, satisfied, she sinks back out of sight to think her thoughts and ponder on the mystery of incubation.

A little after the wrens arrived a fine brown thrasher appeared on the scene. He was all foxy-red and bespotted of breast, and he spent some time investigating a low spot with clumps of saskatoon bushes and rose briers not thirty feet from the window. The window is a large picture one, and without moving or rising I can command a considerable view. I watched the thrasher with great interest as he slunk about in the bushes. Evidently he found things to his satisfaction, for he presently mounted a high twig and announced his claim to the territory with a burst of song.

Next day, by his repeated singing, he enticed a lady thrasher to his bower, and they set to building.

The slope before the cottage is steep, and a shallow, bush-grown ravine deepens towards the bottom. The thrashers take advantage of this, for they always approach from below and reach the nest unseen. When I thought they were well established, I carefully parted the bushes, and there was the nest, close to the ground and containing three eggs as spotted as the birds' breasts. The mother bird crept around among the dead leaves, not allowing me a sight of her, but I heard her harsh, scolding note now from this side, now from that.

By now the robins were hatched, and as I went by for firewood, if I scratched on the shed side, I could see two naked, wobbly heads with enormous gaping mouths waiting blindly for something to be popped in.

My next birds were yellow warblers. I saw the bright male fly to the patch of snowberry fringing the thrashers' bosky home. He disappeared into the two-foot-high shrubs for about five minutes. I could follow his progress by the nodding of the terminal twigs, and guessed he was looking for a convenient fork in which to build a nest.

Early next morning as I sat down to write, I instinctively glanced outside, and I saw the yellow bird's more sober mate glide around the corner of the cottage. Suddenly from mid-air she snatched a piece of poplar-seed gossamer which was floating across the prairie from a nearby bluff. With this in her beak, she flew to the snowberry and disappeared in the greenery. Her mate sang a quick song of joy and then, spying a cobweb at the window corner, he seized this and bore it in triumph away. Another summer home was in the making.

Their nest is of the most exquisite design, at once sturdy and weatherproof, yet as soft as down. I found it after leaving them undisturbed for a week. Having occasion to trim a nearby sapling, a movement caught my eye—a mere flick of leaves—and, following its source, I saw the nest. On looking more closely I saw that it held three warblers' eggs and one larger and darker one—a cowbird's.

I left that egg, for who am I to interfere with nature? The cowbirds were once buffalo birds, and in following the steaming herds had become nomadic, so they leave their eggs to be hatched and their children reared by such good-natured and home-loving creatures as vesper sparrows and yellow warblers. These are among the world's first child-welfare workers. Unlike young cuckoos, a baby cowbird doesn't hoist its foster brothers and sisters from the nest, but tolerates them and becomes the Fat Boy of a happy family.

I am more than lucky with birds. For one thing, I never use

any kind of noxious spray, against either insects or weeds. Many people do; they are townspeople, and they imagine the countryside to be beset with danger, dirt, and disease. They have little time for weeding their flower beds, and have never learnt to live with insects as country folk have. They beat as madly at a harmless moth or a fish fly as they do at a wasp. They are ever ready to hark to the TV advertisements and rush to buy protection from fancied dangers. As a result, many of the birds which nest close to them never raise their young, but die from a diet of poisoned insects.[1] I wonder if the birds know this—and is this why they come so fearlessly to me?

They *do* know more than we think. Only a few days ago—before the robins hatched—a married couple came to visit us. Now, I forgot to warn them that I never passed too close to the robins' nest; not closer than twelve feet. If I did, the mother bird left, and there was danger of the eggs becoming chilled, for the spring wind was cold. But this lady went right up to the nest before I could stop her and, putting her hand against the shed, bent her head to within a foot of the bird. The robin never moved. When I told the lady *I* couldn't have done that, she said, with the rather smug smile that women wear when talking about affairs feminine: "Oh, don't worry! We mothers know each other!"

It is the time of roses. We do not pluck them as we pass, nor do we need to bow our heads to catch their fragrance, for the air is full of it.

A few days ago we had our first June shower, a mere forerunner of the "three-day rains" which the farmers look for at this season. For several days the wind had been in the east, and we saw the clouds slowly gathering, for our rains mostly follow the sun's course.

Already much of the young wheat is up and thirsty, and by the end of the month the last of the crop will be planted, and the farmers must turn their thoughts and their tillage implements towards the land to be summer-fallowed.

Even while the seeds of annual grain crops are germinating, the perennial herbs and wildflowers are already up and doing. Blue beardtongue is common in a rainy June; in dry years it does not flower at all, but simply remains alive. In a few favoured spots we also find its white cousin, which is waxy as a moonstone, with pink centres. One of the more common flowers of the roadside is scarlet mallow, which is more brick-red than scarlet, with prostrate, silvery, and deeply cleft leaves.

We had decided on a trip to the north end of the lake and, following the brief but violent morning shower, we set out. The sun was rapidly drying the dirt road and unlocking all the perfumes of Arabia.

We soon left the graded road and found a prairie trail. This again joined with the "Angling Road." This is an old road that angles straight from Silton Village to the lakeside at Glen Harbour, one of the ports of call for the steamboats in earlier days. Here, on the crest of the hill overlooking the water, is Marieton Church, built years ago by the Anglican settlers hereabouts. The church is tall and white and dignified, and is a landmark for miles around.

Among the headstones in the neat churchyard we found the familiar names, Flavel and Swanston and Wright. One stone bore the simple inscription: "Mother, faithful and true," and nestled beside it was another faithful mother brooding her little family. She was a vesper sparrow, and she sat tight, even as her mate trilled from the churchyard fence.

Today there is development at Glen Harbour, and the summer visitors pass the little church in a cloud of dust, escaping from we know not what—perhaps the fear of death?

"Development" is a word on everybody's lips now. Only the other day a friend of mine told me that he understood I was "developing my property at Pelican Point." I thought I was only painting a small cottage.

Today being Sunday, the parson's car soon arrived, for the church is still served by a faithful priest from Lumsden. Soon the congregation arrived, and we all went in.

Through the open window we could see the great white clouds

marching across the blue, and smell the wolf willow's delicious perfume stealing up from the coulee bank. This shrub is not really a willow (*Salix*), and I believe the botanists classify it as one of the genus *Argentia,* and call it "silver willow"; but all old-timers give it the earlier name, which makes you think that the wolves once denned within its shade.

Wolf willow grows in clumps of varying size and bears tiny yellow blossoms, semi-concealed. Some patches occupy no more than a few square yards; others may spread over several acres. The bushes are anything from three to seven feet tall, and their silvery leaves make a delightful contrast with the ochre-green of prairie grasses and the richer shade of the low, leafy snowberry shrub growing in company with them. Today this exquisite bush is becoming scarcer; the plough has destroyed many acres once overgrown with it, and what remains is confined to pastures and the edges of trails. But as these trails are graded into roads, so the wolf willow is destroyed. Worst of all, the modern craze for "development"—fostered by those who sell the products of the factory—has led to the spraying of this and other low shrubbery wherever it grows in native pastures; the new scientific theory is that such pastures must devote every yard of every acre to grass alone.

The scientists don't ask the older stockmen, ranchers, or farmers; and only these know how many calves and lambs have been kept from chilling in the April winds because of the shelter afforded by these low shrubs. Ride through a patch of snowberry when the wind sweeps down from the North, and you will find many tiny calves curled up, snug and safe and out of sight.

It was the late Archie Budd of the Experimental Station at Swift Current who once said: "There is no substitute for native range." He was not referring only to the shelter afforded by a mixed growth. He also had in mind the steady successions of grasses which mature in a sequence, plus the extra vitamin-rich forbes (asters and other flowering plants), the brouse (willow, poplar, and sages), the fruits of roses, and such extras as mushrooms—all of which are beloved of livestock; all of which added together make up a balanced diet, at once nourishing and tooth-some.

Old range men, who have spent a lifetime following their own grazing herds, observing their preferences and noting their grazing habits, find that considered opinion, based on practical knowledge, is no longer given a hearing. A new generation of experts—geared to the age of technocracy, secure in the degrees they have won in the world of test tubes and scientific research—tell us we are wrong. All of which is most satisfactory to the commercial interests who put up the money for research on chemical sprays, chemical fertilisers, and all the other wonderful aids to nature. The farmer's dollar must not be spent on anything worthwhile of his own choosing; if he is not "progressive" he is not a good citizen—as the salesmen are quick to point out. Neither barons nor serfs died with the Middle Ages—and today our landlord is a book.

Wolf willow may someday be found and smelt only in public gardens, but in the meantime there are still clumps which are the chosen nesting places for such birds as clay-coloured sparrows, whose flat buzz vibrates among the slender, swaying stems, while yellow warblers, kingbirds, and cedar waxwings often weave their nests among the dull purplish twigs.

Sometimes we notice higher, rougher clumps of another silvery-leafed bush. These are buffalo berries, and if you wish to pene-trate their thorny shrubberies you will have to watch yourself. Some of the thorns, which are hardened and pointed terminal twigs, are over three inches long, which is why they were used as needles by the Cree women. Within these fastnesses you may find the nest of a loggerhead shrike or a foxy-red thrasher, or even a mourning dove. Buffalo berry will go too, I expect—but more slowly, for it is indicative of a poor, sandy soil.

I hoped these thoughts were not irreverent, for surely the Creator wants us to understand the value and beauty of all that he has sowed.

The last hymn was sung, and church came out. As we resumed our drive the pipits were singing above the trail, and we stopped the car to look. From our seat on a rock we finally spied a small brown songster pouring forth his tinkling strains. Soon he dropped rapidly to within a few feet of the ground, when he again spread his wings in undulating flight, to dive jerkily into the grass a hundred yards away.

We climbed through the fence of the pasture field and tramped in a circle near the bird's hiding place with no results until, on the point of giving up, a pipit rose at Hope's feet. "Look well!" she called. "I don't dare to move—oh, don't tread on it!" Carefully I parted the grass clumps, and we gazed, silent and rapturous. The tiniest, neatest nest of soft grass; five eggs like small grapes, wine-brown and finely speckled. We tiptoed away, the silvery voice of the Missouri skylark again ringing from the blue void.

So, little by little, with many a pause, we idled along the prairie trail. Soon the last of these trails will be gone, like the wolf willow. Not one mile out of hundreds is left today, for city folk must travel fast wherever they go, and each year they demand more invasion routes, as they seek the unspoilt, which they so soon spoil.

Some indeed keep their little trails—their private nooks—secret, and do not mind travelling slowly and opening gates; but they are few.

"Development" is what sells more equipment, and there must be, it seems, a continual destruction; yet destruction does seem a curious thing on which to base the growth of a country.

A Masai chief in Kenya was asked whether he would sell some of the lovely, lyre-horned cattle which are the riches of his people. It was pointed out to the unlettered African that the stores in Nairobi held a variety of things which the money would purchase. "But," replied the chief, "I know there is nothing in the white man's store one-half as beautiful as my spotted cows. I shall keep them."

Here in Saskatchewan we do not sell our beautiful things directly. We simply bulldoze them out of the way to make room for Progress, the cruel goddess of commercialism. We are seeing the last of our native fauna and flora. A few more generations and "wild" Saskatchewan will be gone.

At the north end of the lake we find a different prairie to what we have traversed. The land is gravelly, treeless, with a low shoreline, for these unploughed levels are raised but a few feet above the water. Much of the lake edge is marshy and cut by the stagnant, winding waterways locally called "the fingers." For the whole flat is a miniature delta where the waters of Wolverine Creek and other small streams unite to feed the lake. These fingers, too, support beds of bullrushes, tule reeds, and three-cornered sedge, backed by tussocks of coarse grass.

Looking south across the open waters you can see the rocky islands, beset with gooseberry bushes, upon which colonies of gulls, terns, and cormorants nest. Till recently the pelicans also bred safely, protected by the waters of this inland sea from prowling dogs and coyotes, but the raising of the level of the lake has sadly embarrassed them; and, although we see some, few of them are now breeding birds.

The reed beds are the places to see and hear birds. Bitterns stalk here at dusk, giving voice to those loud triple notes which suggest a pump at work; "slough pumps," the people call them, because of their habit of excreting as they rise from our feet in that short, flopping, leg-trailing flight which carries them just above the bent reeds to drop down in apparent despair at being so feebly air-borne.

Their cousins, the great blue herons, have much the same long-necked, great-billed outline, but these are no skulkers. They prefer to leave their fishing grounds with a dignified croak, heads well tucked in, legs held at attention and stretched to full length, big wings moving in confident rhythm.

Bubbling marsh wrens creep among the reeds, their oval, well-roofed nests semi-concealed among the large bullrushes. Yellow-headed blackbirds greet us with discordant and jeering notes as they stilt-walk from reed to reed, while the redwings make a brave show in red and black.

Further back, on the dry prairie, the grass is short and wiry, much bespeckled with rose canes and snowberry bush. We heard the flute-like, sadly musical calls of the upland plovers—birds, alas, less common than in early years. We found, however, two nests within a few yards. The birds ran in quick circles, uttering their chattering note—so like a meadow lark's in flight—and occasionally raising and lowering their elegant, sharp wings to show the elongated scapulars. Sandpipers they are, really, which have adopted a plover-like habitat.

We tramped over several wide hollows, where the ground is damper and the grass more lush. Here we heard, but did not see, yellow rails; those very shy and elusive birds which creep through the grass stems as quiet as mice. They can only be located by voice—those sharp, clicking notes which have puzzled so many people. You hear them now to your left, and again to your right; the bird has crossed your path although you didn't see it.

We found to our delight a small colony of bobolinks, and the highlight of the day for Hope was to see several black-and-white males in the air at once, circling on quivering wings and spread tails, bubbling out their rapid yet liquid songs. These wild, sweet notes are not heard often in Saskatchewan; in the Peace River country not at all.

The rich grass carpet here is a riot of wildflowers, chief among them the orange-red prairie lily, our provincial flower emblem, which is so well reproduced on our Administration Building. Like many of our birds, these flowers are disappearing as their habitat shrinks. Bulldozers, ploughs, and—sad to say—the hands of careless people are thinning them out. Tourists halt their cars by the roadside to tear them up. Ninety per cent never even cool their broken stems in water—for they wilt quickly, and children's hot hands hasten the process—so the nosegays are hurled from the moving cars to lie dusty and crushed on the hardtop.

We heard a rumble of thunder and looked up. A mass of cloud, indigo and black and purple, was hurrying towards us from the west. The whole horizon frowned, and the far shore was soon obscured. An occasional eerie streak of greenish, ghoulish white lashed downward, and by that and the billowing appearance of the storm's underbelly we knew that the dark mass was pregnant with hail.

It was as quiet as an empty room. The sun still shone on the marsh as we regained our car, gilding the flatlands till they sparkled beneath the sombre canopy. Then, with a rush of wind, the rain and hail were upon us. The grasses—the lilies—the soft clumps of low willow—were flattened in the instant that the blast struck.

As we hurried down the winding trail the twin tracks filled from the downpour, the water rushing and swirling in a double river. But we had the advantage for the moment, and soon drew far enough south to leave the rain behind. All the northern horizon, we could see, was black as a crow; but, even as we watched, the sun sent a golden shaft through a break in the west, drawing a long pencil line of light across the land; and then to the east, as the storm hushed, we saw God's promise, the bow which joins earth and sky, the bow described by Coleridge as "that gracious thing made up of tears and light" and by Ezekiel as "the likeness of the glory of the Lord."

But the clearing was brief. That night, safe in our beds, we heard a patter on the roof; the longed-for three-day rain had begun.

A few days after the rain, Hope went for her evening walk while I made up my notes. Just after dark she returned, breathless with excitement. "Bobby—foxes!" she cried. "You know that den we found? You said it was a fox den from the tracks— that one along the steep bank? Well—I *saw* them. Five cubs, I think, playing. Then the old dog fox—I think it was—came loping down the bank! I watched them for minutes—it was *adorable!* Oh—and before that—when I was watching the den—I saw a strange bird. It was in that big patch of chokecherry—I'm sure it was a rare bird! Don't laugh at me! It was—let's see—not very large. It had a yellow breast, and a sort of black mark on its cheek—but that's not what I noticed first. It was its *voice!* First it chuckled; then it whistled—loud; then it croaked; all very fast. And it just kept it up till I finally saw it jumping about on the bush. *Is* there any bird that reminds you of?"

I was getting excited too. "It sounds like a chat," I said. "A yellow-breasted chat. It's a kind of relation to the warblers, but larger than most. I saw one once near the Cypress Hills, but this is out of its range—if it *is* one. We'll investigate tomorrow."

And investigate we did. He started his hullabaloo as soon as we got within a hundred yards of his bush. He had a wife, and after a long and careful search (one must not break the bushes), we found the rough little nest of twigs and bents complete with five elegantly spotted eggs.

Surely this is the furthest north and east that a chat has been recorded in Saskatchewan. They are birds of the semi-arid prairie to the south, and the few records we have for this province are from the White-Mud River area of the High Plains and from the South Saskatchewan River badlands—stragglers from the breaks of the Missouri River in Montana and South Dakota.

The find was a fitting climax to the fabulous month of June.

CHAPTER IV

July—The Moon of Games

The first of July found me, at an early hour, on the bank above the lake. I sat unmoving among some low shrubbery watching through my field glasses a pair of yellow warblers feeding their young.

Earlier still, I had been sketching.

Below me a speedboat cut the water on its way north, leaving a great wake which lapped the shoreline noisily. Around the bend the boat must have stopped for the noise of its motor ceased. These voyagers would, I guessed, be dedicated fishermen, using the "angle" which is almost as old as man. At the end of an hour they returned, but slowly, with the motor closed down to a quiet mutter; and I saw they were, indeed, angling.

I heard them talking, these two men. Voices carry upward from the water for a remarkable distance, and although they were a good quarter of a mile away they might, to my ears, have been at my elbow.

One said: "Look! Someone's watching us from the bank—I wonder what for?"

The other cocked an eye. "Some snoopy guy, I guess. Well, if it's the Game Warden we should worry—we've got licenses." And he turned his back.

After a while the first spoke again. "No," he said. "It's not *us* he's watching. He's looking through his glasses at something. Wait, I know—he's one of them crazy bird watchers!"

These two men soon landed with their fish. They passed close to me, and we said good morning.

"What's that?" one said, seeing my open sketchbook on the

grass. "Oh, I see—flowers, eh? My wife uses a colour film. Gee, she gets some swell photographs, doesn't she, Jim? You should see them. And, say, you ought to see the flowers at our place—I mean real flowers! My wife's petunias are pretty good, if you want to paint flowers—and it won't be long before the gladiolas are out."

I thanked him for his interest, feeling that the tall-stemmed, purple burgamots I had sketched were but weeds to him.

Many of the cottage people are devoted gardeners as well as fishermen, and spend long, healthy hours beautifying their grounds, bringing roots and seeds from their city homes; yet somehow what makes for beautiful surroundings in the environment of bricks and mortar seems a little false—a little out of place—at the beach, like fussy ornaments on the walls of a log house.

Some of my visitors gently plead with me to tear up "those awful weeds" as they have done, to make room for flower beds. My awful weeds are clumps of soft, sweet-smelling sage; and brittle, bright-flowered cactus; and wild rose bushes, and tight little clumps of yellow prairie parsley, as well as blue beard-tongue and soft, feathery annual willow herb like pink lace, and these are all disposed about my half-acre of pristine hillside in that artless and charming arrangement which the hand of man sometimes imitates but rarely achieves.

The grassy slopes with their lichened rocks and wildflowers suit my taste very well. I never wished for trees on grasslands, or grasslands in the forest. We may have to alter these things for survival, but I see no other reason for our trying to "improve" on nature.

Certainly this hilltop is windy, but I love the wind-swept places. There is a kinship between them, a bond between, say, the Sussex downs and the Saskatchewan prairies, between fog-damped moors and the high plateaus of the Cypress Hills, which is something more than topographical.

The pale cowslips of the downs are close to earth, like our prairie crocuses, and the dotterels of the Perthshire Highlands differ but little from our delightful mountain plovers.

Plains, valleys, hills—I love them all. But especially the hills, the open hills, where the upward-sweeping wind gives a buoyancy to our cumbersome bodies and wings to our souls.

There is hope in hills. Couched in blue against the far horizon, they seem like giants who, having overcome the quicksands and marish bogs of the low places, now lie at rest in utter tranquility. The eagles and the curlews know them as they knew them in the long ago. Surely when the psalmist raised his eyes unto the hills he heard the one and saw the other.

Many of us have known the swamps and the fetid jungles of life; but always, when we parted the noxious growth, we caught a glimpse of the bright sky, and saw the dim outline of the heights for which our souls had longed. Happy, twice happy, are those who have always dwelt in the high and lofty places.

Weeds are supposed to be plants out of place. In this sense even a garden flower can be a weed, and certainly some—like kochia—delight to find their freedom, and will spread far and wide.

Yet weeds have their uses. They are not cause, but effect; when we bulldoze away the topsoil, the weeds come, and they are the cover crop for grass. They are part of a necessary cycle of which the end result is a natural climax, best suited to conditions. Forest takes over once more if land in wooded countries is left fallow and unworked. Grass will take over on abandoned prairie lands. But first must come shrubbery to shade the young trees, and weeds to nurture the grass.

People hate weeds; they say they are untidy. So they spray them, spreading noxious substances which may adversely affect ourselves. Others pull them by hand, and wonder why the grass seeds they plant wither and die in the hot sun, and why the bank itself washes away.

The farmers are all working their summer fallow now. The idea of fallow is old. It is mentioned in the Bible as a necessary part of good husbandry: "For in the seventh year there shall be a Sabbath of rest for the land." To give this rest is the main purpose, but secondary reasons are to "clean" the land by eliminating weeds,[1] while at the same time the working of the soil and keeping down of growth conserves moisture from summer rain and winter snow.

Modern methods of handling summer fallow are different from the old way, which aimed to "keep the summer fallow black." That was the slogan which passed from lip to lip and was printed in every farm journal in the 1920's. The Agricultural Departments sent out literature on the need for constantly working the fallow land. The makers of farm implements brought out new and better machines for doing this. Another slogan said: "Each stroke of the harrows is another two bushels per acre."

Alas, when the dry years came, the overpulverized soil—ploughed, disced, harrowed, worked every time a few green weeds appeared—lost its humus, and the big winds of the 1930's lifted the dried soil by tons and swept it away.

A farmer said to his wife: "Well, Mary, we should have a bumper crop next year; the summer fallow is like an onion bed." But next spring they were to see the roadway blocked with dirt and find nothing of the faithful gangplough but the levers sticking up above a packed drift of topsoil.

If the farmer is still, today, a little suspicious, a little slow to adopt the advice of some farm expert, perhaps he has reason.

Nowadays one of their big cries is to break up all native pasture, grub out all bluffs and patches of brush, and seed these down to pasture mixtures. The value of natural growth is hardly recognised, in spite of the words of the late Archie Budd which I have already quoted. He once told me that even he could not speak too plainly or openly about many things with which he was not in favour, because as a civil servant he was obliged to follow the policy of the day. And, while he did not say what that policy was at any given time, reading between the lines I gathered that he meant a policy of going along with the world of commerce which handles forage crop seeds, special implements for sowing

and harvesting, new fertilisers and legume inoculators, and—
above all—heavy machinery for the destruction of brush cover.[2]

At tremendous expense experts have scoured central Asia for
grasses which, in spite of being highly desirable—like crested
wheat grass—in a limited way, are no better, if as good, as our
native buffalo grass, fescues, and wheat grasses—and certainly
not as permanent.

Mr. Budd told me that he had tried, but failed, to interest the
department in harvesting seed from stands of these native grasses
for use in regrassing abandoned areas.

Unfortunately, Mr. Budd—one of our best field botanists—did
not have the now coveted degree which alone gives backing to
any statement. In spite of which, after many years when his
actual status was not much above that of a labourer, he received
shortly before his death long-overdue recognition by way of
honoris causa; but dead men let out no secrets.

On the livestock front we are also beset with any amount of
advice which, if followed, will make money for veterinary supply
companies, druggists, and laboratory workers. Some of the products and methods are fine, but many others are of doubtful value,
and we cannot see their ultimate end. Certainly the cost is
enough, first by way of taxes to support the experimental work
and then by what we pay for the results.

Artificial insemination is a case in point; just because it has
been proved possible, just because it is widely used, are no more
arguments for it than the fact that it is possible to get drunk, and
hundreds do.

Granted, a lot of people get enjoyment from using new things;
they hate to stand still. That is, of course, the danger of the
Bomb—someone will want to use it. The effect of the Bomb will
be instantaneous, and the user will see what it does; but it may
take many years—possibly hundreds—before we know the ultimate result of what is a violation of nature. Perhaps sterility will
be one.

Surely the act of procreation was not meant to be accomplished by mechanical means? Surely there is something akin to human love, of togetherness of the spirit, in the mating even of what we call the beasts of the field? Nature, outraged, may be slow—but she may be very sure of her revenge.

Then we have the implanting of female hormones into male animals to de-sex them and make them fatten more readily. We cannot yet calculate what effect this may have on the humans who eat the meat.

We have tenderizers and meat colourings now, and Heaven knows what the next few years will bring.

If human infants can be born cripples by the use of modern drugs, are we to think that the animals will be more carefully considered?

Perhaps the farmers and ranchers will someday be trusted to use their own practical knowledge of nature to supply us with good, wholesome food, but it is doubtful. Manipulation, expert advice, and vertical integration have gone too far, and few men will quarrel with their bread-and-butter so long as the poison in the slice works slowly enough.

Be that as it may, it is good to see that farmers no longer burn stubble, and that they do not use the plough overmuch, but rather use deep cultivation methods which leave the land rough and keep enough trash on the surface to hold the soil together when the strong winds of spring come out of the west.

This is a stony country. The stones are of various sizes, colours, and kinds. There are granites both large and small in reds and greys and blues; quartz in glittering whites and pinks, and great white limestones, some weighing tons, cracked and seamed, easily flaked off in layers two to six inches thick.

Some of the larger granite rocks stand several feet high, worn to a smooth patina and surrounded by a trough-like depression. These were the rubbing stones of the buffalo herds, and some are still used by cattle. Here the humpbacked beasts found solace from the itchiness of their faded winter coats as they loosened and peeled under the warm sun of spring, and it was the cloven hooves of these wild cattle which stamped out the encircling trenches.

They had a defence against flies, too, and you can still see on unploughed land the hollows dug by these animals with horns and hooves, throwing the dry dust over their shoulders, or sometimes lying in the cool dirt safe from their stinging tormentors. Buffalo wallows, we call these shallow depressions which the prairie years and the prairie grasses are reclaiming.

The stones are beautiful to the eye, but a sore trial to the husbandman, for they dull his blades and break his low-hung harvesting equipment. Great piles in the fields and loose scatterings along the fencelines, give evidence of the back-breaking labour involved in removing the large ones with a crowbar, chain, and team in the early days.

I remember when families of half-breeds—many from the old métis settlement of Willow Bunch—used to travel about with their wagons, tents, and loose horses, engaging to dig and pick rocks at so much a cord. We do not see them on the road now—the Trottiers, the Dumonts, the La Plantes. Usually they worked on untouched prairie, for the surface rock had to be removed before the breaking plough of those days could be used. Indians also did a lot of this work, besides which they built miles of fences, cut hundreds of cords of firewood, stooked many acres of grain, and worked on the threshing gangs.

But that work has gone. The Indians learned the arts of the white man of those days, when the settlers themselves were working men. But the Indian used his acquired skill only briefly, and now he is even further behind us than he was at the time of the Treaties. Just as we destroyed his hunting culture so, later, we destroyed his new means of livelihood; and today there is no place for him. He, loving freedom, worked by contract, and he sees only misery in a future demanding that work be done by the clock, requiring a high school education which, within a few years, will still leave him behind as technocracy installs more automation.

Of all the sorrows we have heaped upon our red brothers,

from taking his hunting grounds to forbidding him the right to say how he may spend his few dollars, nothing equals in downright wickedness our leaving him with idle hands. The "Indian problem" is the white man's sin.

Limestone is only a nuisance today. Once it was not so. Only a mile north of our cottage is a lime pit in which early settlers burned the stones to make mortar. Quite a few stone houses were built, and many chimneys made, in the day when the railway was far away and the miles long.

For those first settlers who had the knack of understanding their environment, the prairies provided bounteously. Some built with poplar logs—neat, tight little homes, cool in summer, warm in the lamp-lit winter. About Last Mountain, in the hills to the east and along the valley, there were plenty of poplar trees large enough for this, but elsewhere the poles were small; however, even they were used, plentifully daubed with mud within and without.

On the bare, treeless prairies the homesteaders ploughed the thick, strong sod of the slough sides, and made warm, roomy houses which defied the blast of any blizzard, and in which red geraniums could sit in the deeply embrasured windows without fear of freezing.

A few people lived in dugouts clawed out of a steep coulee side, roofed with brush or sod and walled up in front with rough lumber.

But here in the Silton district a less common material was used for home building. It was clay, and many of these so-called "mud" houses are in use today, their two-foot-thick walls lined within and sheathed outside with good, painted lumber. They were made in this way: First, on a patch of high ground the surface sod was ploughed up and removed; this exposed a layer of white clay, which was again ploughed and reploughed. Water was then hauled in barrels and dumped in the pit, together with prairie hay, to form a binding medium. The mass was tramped with horses until of the correct adhesive consistency.

When the building site had been cleared of sod, and the outline of the house marked out, the clay was shovelled in between retaining boards, just as in cement work. When the first round—about a foot high—was almost dry, the boards were raised and the process repeated until the eaves were reached. In putting on the roof, it was important to provide wide eaves to protect the walls from the rain, which might otherwise cause disintegration.

The whole procedure resembles the making of the *muttee* buildings familiar to travellers in India and other eastern countries. The mud forts of the Hill Rajahs of which Kipling wrote were built this way, and one wonders whether the idea was brought here from the East—for certainly men who had served in India were among our early settlers.[3]

It seems a pity that we must now pay enormous prices for synthetic building supplies of all kinds—metals, woods, and plastics—while what grows on our own acres, what we must pay taxes on, is so much waste. And the satisfying arts of man are lost.

One day by the beach I found the rusted head of a broadaxe. None of my beach neighbours knew what it was, but I had used one in my early days for squaring the roof joists of a log building. I keep it, for it reminds me of another of the arts of man; of a people who could tie the fisherman's knot as it was tied on the shores of Galilee, or twist the sheaf band that Ruth knew; who knew how to burn white poplar for lye, to mix with it the tallow of their own beasts to produce the strong white soap we used. A few women still do this, but it is a passing art.

The harness "horse" stands neglected in the shed, and people nowadays wonder what it is, or what is a wax end, or how to sew a trace. Indeed, only recently I was in a hardware store and asked the young man in charge for a sewing awl; not only did he not have one, but—worse still—he did not know what an awl was, although I pronounced the name with a long "a," a short "a," and an "or," and sketched a picture of it, as I explained its use.

The very names of things are forgotten, although they live on the printed page; but who reads Wordsworth or Coleridge or Longfellow now? Perhaps we should have a special dictionary to preserve nouns like *frail* (which is a tool bag) and *bucket* and *yoke* and *besom* and *tine* and *hame*. Do you know what a *throat latch* is, or a *stone boat,* or a *go-devil* or a *churn dash* or a *gambrel stick?* The clever hands of man made these things with cunning, used them with care—those things which had beauty because each contained in itself the brains, the blood, the heart-beats of one man or woman.[4]

We yearn dumbly for we know not what, and so today we have the artsy-craftsy crowd who don't even know the reason for the artsy-craftsy things they make at the adult education courses subsidized by government to still those yearnings and bring "culture" to the land.

Today only our northern Indians still know the joy of a stick picked from the wood, the bark stripped from a tree, the roots dug from a muskeg, and the pitch taken from a pine—all within a few rods of camp—each selected at leisure, looked at, stroked with a sensitive thumb, tested and tried. And from these the Indian will build a canoe—light for transportation over the rough portages, water-worthy against the sudden squalls which blow up on our northern lakes; a canoe beautiful in outline, in soft colour, in texture, in smoky smell, in quick gliding motion, and silent as the great trees from which it came.

The Indian will still want to tell his story while the bannock bakes—the story of his canoe; to teach his children, as he was taught, the story of the woman who is a birch tree, of how she weeps when cut, of how the squaw must take the sap and say: "See, woman, these are your tears; they are not wasted, for the Great Spirit sees you."

But there are none to hear the tale, for the children are learning fractions and grammar and rock-'n'-roll; and they put on lipstick and silk stockings and high heels, because they are ashamed of their dark hair and darker eyes and the fullness of their lips.

If you have not seen a well-built house of logs or prairie sod, if you have not seen a birchbark *chemaun* or a *wapooswyan,* you have missed real beauty, and you have not seen the underpainting of Canada. The logs are rotting, the canoes are few, rabbit robes take time to make, cattle rub on the ruins of the soddy, and the dust of the hut blows unheeded across the fields, to mingle again with the Earth Mother who holds the bones of the builders.

The intellectuals of an urbanized world will not readily understand the countryman's devotion to the soil, in the way that the squires of pre-industrial days did. Just as the landowners of England made the mistake of their lives in flirting with new industrial concepts, so today the uneasy alliance, within a political party, of farmers and the labour unions can bode no good for the freedom of husbandry.

I am not theorizing. I am a countryman. I have been in turn squire's grandson, artist's son, labourer (what else is a hired man?), peasant (what else is a homesteader?) and landowner— a rancher of many wide acres. I have had to use my environment. I have known the joy of the burden and the heat of the day; the joy of that independence from manufactured things by which one sees a bench in a spruce tree and a wagon tongue in a birch— and one knows that it takes but the axe and the saw to effect the transformation.

I know what it is to plough and sow and reap and mow and be a farmer's boy, as the old song says.

But rural development, rural planning, and the other pet theories of the technocrat are not quite on the same basis, and the countryman's heart does not speak as it did; while the farmer's boy has become the tourist, returning to the land that his grandfather pioneered to shoot the birds, uproot the trees, and murder the flowers. Grandfather didn't know much.

The hot days of July are enjoyed to the full by the cottage folk. Now that the holidays are here, the women and children stay all week. Some husbands, too, take their holidays now, to relax and fish and boat and join in the water sports. All day and far into the night you hear the roar of outboard motors and turbo-jets above the merry cries of children.

Everyone is getting berry-brown, and appetites are simply enormous. It is fine that there should be places where these people can get rid of the atmosphere of the city—although it is true that to some extent they bring it with them.

Children often come knocking at the door to chat with Hope, and pretty they look, the little girls and boys, so freckled and sunburnt, swinging their brown legs as they sit in a row on the couch gravely discussing the latest stars of the world of pop music.

One bigger girl with pale golden hair borrows books, for she is a great reader and can lose herself for hours in *Little Women* or *Jo's Boys*.

Sometimes we all play together, but not for long. The call of the lake is too strong, and while the tiny ones paddle the near teen-agers take turns on the water skis amid ecstatic shrieks.

"In June he changes his tune," says an old verse about cuckoos —but this referred to the European bird, which here only pops out of clocks. Our American bird, the black-billed cuckoo, is more consistent, and still repeats his *cuck-uk-cou* well into July. These interesting birds seem to be more common of late years—why, I cannot imagine. They are like mourning doves, of comparable size and similar habitat, and we certainly see and hear them much more often than in early days.

These cuckoos are not parasitic like their European cousins, but are content to build their own nests—albeit shoddily—and raise their families.

The chokecherry shrubbery is often their chosen place for a nest, but they are shy birds, and their secret is not easily un-covered. The flight of the cuckoo is graceful and silent. He flits from grove to grove in the most unobtrusive way, but perch-ing he swings his long and beautifully marked tail like a pendulum, and this is what will be most likely to attract the eye, for his olive-brown upper parts and dull white breast make him otherwise inconspicuous, especially for so large a bird, for with his sweeping tail he looks larger than a robin. If you are lucky enough to sit perfectly still, he may alight close enough to show you the handsome ring of red about his eye.

The mourning doves are bolder. Flying, they clap their wings like tame pigeons. As they walk on the road you may see their dove-grey, slightly sheeny plumage and notice their coral-red feet. They, too, nest in the shrubby or low trees, and their building attempts are even more shoddy than the cuckoo's; and, while the latter's eggs are richest blue-green, the dove's are pure white, with just a tinge of pink from the yolk within.

As July draws to a close the cuckoo's voice ceases altogether, but the doves still salute the evening air in pleading accents of *woe-o-woe*.

The wheat is in bloom, and gives off a sweet odour which surrounds us as we listen to the doves. The hot air is cooling, and the wheat smell is mingled with the scent of dry roadside dust, of ripening grass, of sage essence and yarrow, and the pungent, sneezy smell of ragweed.

The grasshoppers are in full cry now, and the warm hillsides are fairly jumping with them. The gulls come in thousands, flocking to feast on the noisy throng. The crows, too, walk the slopes in little cawing groups, snatching now here, now there, as they gorge themselves.

Towards evening the gulls gather up, passing high above the cottage as they weave their way north; should it be windy they drop down almost to the lake, and the long lines beat steadily on.

The sun sets blood-red. Indeed, he has been red all day, for the air is heavy and redolent of the bush fires which are burning two hundred miles north, somewhere above Prince Albert. The north wind has brought this haze, which fills the hollows like water, and with it the smell of burning spruce and willow and the dry peat of the muskegs, like the smell of smoke-tanned Cree moccasins. This distillation of the northland may obscure our prairie horizon for many days yet—or till the wind changes.

And so to bed, while from the open window the grasshoppers

still shrill, and the crickets are not far behind. Are they reciting an ancient saga, with no beginning and no end, like the *Om mani padme om* of a Tibetan at prayer? Are they repeating, at the behest of the Great Spirit, a medicine song in praise of life and love?—a song born on Creation's Great Day, long since forgotten by man?

Perhaps an Indian might know, but he will not say, for there is wisdom in silence.

CHAPTER V

August—The Moon of Berries

August is the month of ripening or reaching full growth. The Indians call it the moon-of-flying-from-the-nest.

We are reminded daily of this ripening, for wild fruit is everywhere, except where late frosts rendered barren the blossoms of May.

The saskatoons—and, indeed, the wild strawberries—came to full colour and flavour earlier, and what remain on the shrubs and vines are now withered. But the pin cherries, the choke-cherries, and the buffalo berries are just coming into their season, and the bush cranberries will not be far behind.

The city folk are out picking wherever there are laden bushes easily accessible by car. At one time the Indian women peddled their dew-fresh berries from door to door, and we haggled for them at so much a basketful, with the birchbark basket or *weaganis* thrown in to boot; but since the cars came, people can drive far and wide, and find their own berry patches—sometimes with scant regard for property rights and the feelings of the busy farmers' wives.

But the Indians are still the principal harvesters of buffalo berries, which we hate to pick because of their wicked thorns. The Indians travel by wagon—perhaps more often now by truck —and camp near the clumps of thick-set, dull-grey bushes, pitching their tents in some sheltered spot. It used to be a common sight in the sand hills about Battleford to see the smoke-browned top of a tipi projecting above the shrubbery—but these lodges are rarer now, and a small canvas tent is in common usage.

They do not attempt to pick the berries by hand as we do.

Rather, they cut off the heavily laden boughs with sharp little axes. These are piled high in the wagon and drawn to camp. Here the girls spread them on blankets and beat them with small sticks to dislodge the fruit. Then the empty branches are put aside, the blanket is picked up at the four corners, and the harvest is tossed sharply up and down in the wind. This soon carries away the small twigs and leaves and thorns, leaving only the clean winnowed berries to lie in a neat red heap in the centre of the blanket. These berries are usually dried, and then used in winter to knead into "sweet bannock." This operation apparently does no harm to the bushes; on the contrary, the Indians say they bear the better for this pruning.

The whites turn this fruit into jelly, and buffalo jelly is one of Saskatchewan's finest dainties, only surpassed in flavour by jelly from the guilder rose—the bush cranberry which flourishes in the dark coulees.

The birds and the chipmunks both compete with us for these small fruits; the chipmunk, always; the birds less now than later—for there is still plenty of insect food. Eventually the young robins, the thrashers, and the cedar waxwings will plunder the boughs, and much later the migrating finches will gorge themselves as they pass on their southward journey.

And whatever is left to dry and hang desiccated through the winter will be gleaned by the pine grosbeaks and bohemian waxwings when the snow lies deep. Coyotes and foxes, badgers and skunks and ground squirrels, all will pluck fruit from the lower boughs, or pick the fallen; but—as every child knows—the high hung fruit is too sour even for foxes.

The chipmunks dearly love the pointed fruit of pin-cushion cactus. The early hillsides were adorned with the rich, reddish purple of this prickly plant, but now it too has ripened to a fruit as sweet as honey. You must squeeze it gently on the tongue to get the full, cool flavour; but if you are not alert for the ripening, the saucy rodents will have stolen a march on you and eaten it all.

Pin cherries make a clear, pale-red jelly which is firm and sweet and much valued by prairie housewives.

But it is the heavy-bearing and ubiquitous chokecherry which supplies the greater part of the needs of rodents and birds. Even cattle will pluck them. When fully ripe the berries are almost black, very glossy, and they hang in clusters so heavy that the slender branches are borne down by their weight. Cooked with plenty of sugar they are delicious, with a wild, astringent taste. They will not "jell" without added pectin, but make into a thick, purplish syrup which is a treat of treats for pouring over hot cakes or fresh-baked bread—quite the equal, to my palate, of the maple syrup of Quebec.

The lovely little bunches of opaque, greenish-white snowberries we do not eat. They, too, hang—or, I should say, remain, for they do not hang *down*—for a long time on the low, woody shrubs, and are beloved of the few prairie chickens which now remain.

Once, long ago, there were bears treading this lakeshore for fish and these coulee banks for berries, as there are in the North today. These animals fattened on berries in anticipation of the cold weather, which in the weeks to come would force them to take to their dens and suck their claws till spring.[1] White women would not want to meet these shaggy plantigrades in the berry patch, but the women of the Crees show little fear, knowing that they can easily put their shaggy "ancestor" to flight with hard words and well-aimed sticks.

Throughout the year there are many sources of food and drink on these "barren plains," as they have been miscalled; wild onions, wild carrots, mushrooms, dandelion roots (from which you can make good coffee), the various berries I have named and others which I have not. The Indians knew and used them all. They used nettle tops for greens (as we have done). They made tea from raspberry canes and from prairie sage. They knew the value of rose hips (as cattle do, too) and the fruit of haw-thorns. In the wooded parts they had wild sarsaparilla, seneca root, and the delicious fungus we call morels. They made birch tea from the fine twigs of that tree, and used the gushing sap too.

They made spruce tea, and a warming drink from the shrub we call Labrador tea. They taught these arts to us, but some we already knew; we had long made dandelion wine, and we used most of the mushrooms, too, like the bracket fungus, which grows out of tree trunks like great oyster shells all in layers.

Once, at Meeting Lake, three hundred miles and many years removed from Silton, I stopped at the rude shack of a settler from Hungary. The man had been clearing bushland, and acres of clean-cut stumps and great piles of limbs and twigs showed how mightily he had laboured. He asked me to stay for dinner, and he told me about his early life in "old contree," as his smiling, brown-faced wife gave the last stirs to the big pot before serving from it.

"Yes, meesta, it takes lotsa vork makit new land. Ve gotta eat lots. Meat you need, lots meat." The woman filled my bowl with a semi-liquid, savoury mess with chunks of chicken-like white meat.

My host finally said, wiping his wide cavalry moustache (he had been a Hussar) with the back of his hand: "You know what iss you eat?"

I said, "No."

He got up, reached in the corner by the woodbox, and produced a great bracket fungus. "Dis iss meat for poor mans," he said, and grinned and threw it back in the corner. "Old contree ve eat it. Ve vork hard, too. When I come this contree I see. I say, 'Mama, now I can vork—ve got meat, see?'"

So much for the nutritive value of something to be found in every forest, but so rarely noticed.[2] These Europeans boil it for hours in milk, then they strain off the milk and add cream, salt, and paprika.

The "dusty millers" are active this month, and are much attracted by the oil lamp by which I write. They get in the house somehow, and are constantly committing suicide in the lamp chimney, but as a preliminary to their death plunge they like to walk over my white paper and blot the ink. Hope likes me to catch them carefully and put them outside, but they fare little better there, for they flutter at the window, and sometimes a small bat swoops, and *snick-snack!*—he bites off the insect's wings and drops low to the ground as he secretes it in his little tail pocket to take home and eat at leisure.

Nighthawks are after the same morsels as they dive and wheel, and all through the dusk their *pee-it* notes are heard—now far, now near.

Once under a street light in Silton we found a great, furry polyphemus moth. It had newly emerged from the chrysalis, and was clinging to a shed to dry its new wings. Slowly it opened and shut those beautiful wings, all gold-dusted, with the eye spot such as we see on a peacock's tail, all the time waving its fringed antennae. Finally we left for home, but the next day we saw those lovely ochre-grey wings lying amputated on the sidewalk—either a bat or a nighthawk, or possibly even a skunk, preferred meat to beauty.

There are several sulphur butterflies about. They haunt the sun-drenched hillside, and are attracted to the newly opened, purple-red flowers of the blazing stars which stud the browning August grass. It always amazes me that these dry, hot prairies can nurture such an exotic-looking flower.

The many varieties of goldenrod and asters do not, somehow, surprise me in the same way. These are tall, strong plants, deep-rooted, and they appear well able to take care of themselves, no matter how the bitter winds blow. Also, they seek, to some extent, the shelter of the bluff fringes and the shrubby roadsides where they are somewhat protected.

But the blazing star stands solitary, not supported by brothers and sisters, but apart on the stony knolls where it must compete with the hardy grasses. Yet it blooms on and on; up to eighteen inches high in a wet year, and perhaps no more than six or eight if the rains are stingy.

There is much movement going on among the garter snakes. Every day we see one or more. Always they are working downhill in the direction of the lake. With the dry weather many sloughs have shrunk to brown mud, and these are water-loving snakes. They are facile swimmers, and we often see them in the water when it is calm, their heads and perhaps six to eight inches of their necks protruding above the surface, like flower stalks, the sun shining on the inset gems which are their eyes.

Later, of course, they will gather together to hibernate in some cranny or cutbank where, twined together, they will lie torpid till spring. I remember seeing one such gathering or "ball" of snakes, thanks to Old Jimmy Duiguid. Jimmy was an Aberdonian with whom I once neighboured. He had been a house carpenter at Balmoral Castle when Victoria was Queen. He would tell me tales of the "Auld Leddy" (whom he revered); of her kindness and thoughtfulness to the staff. She may not have been always amused by the speech and actions of those who should have known better, but she was prepared to make plenty of allowances for those who had not had advantages.

Jimmy had a homestead which he sometimes visited, but mostly he did job carpentry all over the country, moving from place to place on foot quite happily.

One late fall day he came to my place. "Laddie," he said, "if ye'll just gie me a bed and tak' me wi' my groceries to the homestead in the morn', I'll be obliged till ye." So next day I took him by wagon to his little wooden house, which was built against the side of a coulee bank "forbye the wind doesna' shriek at me there, and the wee spring's by the door." Homestead shacks are never locked, and he pushed in the door and bade me enter, for, he said, we'd have a cup o' tea.

While the kettle boiled we noticed a bulge in the half-rotten wall of half-inch lumber and poles which lined the bankside of the dwelling. Saying he'd best tear away the broken boards to replace them, Old Jimmy took hold of a cracked edge and pulled. With a sharp crack and a cloud of dust, a chunk of wall several feet wide came away—and with it, a monstrous ball of snakes fully three feet across. Jimmy jumped on the table, I on a rickety chair. The writhing, hideous mass rolled to the door jamb and began to resolve itself into single snakes, double (joined) snakes, triple snakes, heads staring in all directions like Medusa's tresses. These finally untangled themselves. The reptiles glided round and round like participants in an underworld ballet, till one finally reared its head over the doorstep and followed with its coiling body. Others followed, till presently they had all left, and we could hear only dry rustlings in the fallen leaves of the coulee bottom.

"Losh me!—'tis a lot o' sairpents!" was all Old Jimmy said, and just then the kettle boiled as a last salute to the Powers of Darkness.

The dumping (or "nuisance") ground reserved for dwellers at Pelican Point is two miles up the road. Here at a crossroads corner once stood a country school. The schoolhouse itself has gone—hauled away in the craze for centralization. Consolidation is perhaps the more correct word in this case, I suppose. But the once trim caragana hedge remains as a nesting place for gold-finches and mourning doves, together with two spruce trees once lovingly set and nurtured by the children of the last generation. These dark trees, once planted in high hopes, are lonely now—they miss the boys and girls—but they still serve a useful purpose as a landmark. I invariably tell my friends who are not familiar with the road to Pelican Point: "Drive west till you see two lone spruce trees at a crossroads; there, turn south, and the road brings you to my cottage."

"Consolidation" has sadly altered the rural scene, and in addition to the schoolhouses which have been uprooted and hauled to towns, many others stand forlorn by the road, with broken windows and peeling paint and doors slamming idly in the prairie wind. The gophers run in and out, little heeding the arithmetic problem still chalked on the blackboard by a vanished hand.

Of course, these changes have meant money to the commercial world in a day when economists press us to discard the hard-won things which we built and love, in order always to buy or build something new; in these days when a dollar saved is thought to be five dollars lost—hence our national and provincial debt.

"Consolidation" meant money in many ways besides to the building trade. "A better standard of living" for the teacher meant she must buy more *things*. What need had the old-time dedicated teacher for a car? Many were happy enough to remain as members of the community. They did not find it necessary to leave each weekend and holiday.

One of the results of the new order will not make itself felt for some time; it is that children are losing touch with the rural environment which should be their happy birthright. No longer do they walk or gallop their ponies to school, for they are taken to town in a bus. And a bus does not reckon miles by stone piles, or gullies, or culverts where the weasels hide; or by the grooves of wagon tires, or hoofprints; or by the birds' nests found, or spotted frogs admired—but by a mechanical device of figures and fractions enclosed under glass.[3]

Nor does the bus know in which direction the Milky Way lies, or the movements of the Great Plough or the location of the North Star.

The bus just follows the road, and it has no recollection of previous trips or memory of its driver's forefathers, who travelled here on many a black and moonless night, in many a screeching blizzard, finding their way by their sixth sense and that of their horses. These men and their horses had that sense which knows by instinct in what direction home lies, that sense which calculates the miles by hills and ravines, and the way by the direction of the wind, by how the snowdrifts are banked or how the grass lies. These men knew whether their wagon wheels were on the trail or on the untracked prairie by the *feel,* and they came and went alike on the black nights, or when the stars guided them home.

In two wars the Canadian troops possessed something which was the envy of other armies; a combination of initiative, learned around the farm, and a sense of direction learned in the school of the outdoors.

This will be lost, I suppose—but perhaps it doesn't matter.

They say there will be no more wars, as they have said dozens of times. *The Voice of Women* doesn't even want children to have toy soldiers any more. Hideous "Barbie" dolls are, I suppose, officially approved. Better think of new clothes, even if Barbie will have no one to defend her. In England she is "Cindy"—invented to make children clothes-conscious customers. So does commercialism thrive at the expense of childhood.

But progress continues. Where once the repetitions of the three R's flooded from the open window in the sound of eager, childish voices, where once the Union Jack fluttered and the recess bell tolled, there is now only a great ugly hole made by a bulldozer.[4] A malodorous hole into which we throw our trash and fish guts. A hole buzzing with flies, in which we saw once a badger, bloody-headed, and a great horned owl. They lay, these two, stinking and corrupt, the eyes of the owl still open and glaring defiance in death, the badger supine, bloated, and a thing of no consequence for all the powerful digging claws, the short, muscled arms. Funny (what a word!) that we should destroy a living creature just because *we* don't want it. And they will not let us play with toy soldiers! We do not grow wise very fast. It saddens me. It is of no use to be angry.

I have cracked my skull on too many bureaucratic walls to hope for any change in those who have charge of—have life or death over—our wild relations. The noble idea of conservation based on a right to live has fallen through. We shall continue to please the money grubbers. We shall continue to sell the eatable like so much pork sausage, and allow the uneatable no rights; they have no place in a planned economy. An Indian would at least have supped on both the owl and Old Brock—or left them alone. It is a part of a new religion wherein man, not God, is lord, answerable to no one but himself.

We are not without domestic stock at our cottage, and a great joy they are to us, for so much of our lives were spent on the cattle ranges. These are Angus cattle, a good-sized herd which pastures in late summer in a field separated only by a fence from our property. While not legally ours—for they belong to a young farmer who lives with his sister some four miles away—while they do not bear my brand, they are nevertheless ours to enjoy, to watch, and I am sure our aesthetic possession of them causes no loss to my neighbour and he does not begrudge us.

We love to see the sleek, black cows come in single file down the steep hill paths to drink, each with its lusty calf at foot. We love to see these calves gambol and play together while the mothers slake their thirst, pausing between whiles to turn dripping, anxious muzzles towards their charges in mute promise of a quick return.

Sometimes these cattle bed down in the long grass near the fence, on a spot below our cottage and nearer to the lake. Another cottage occupies this lower level, and the proximity of these cattle at such times is a source of irritation to these good people when in residence. "Nasty smelly things," they say. "The Government should do something about it. One might as well live next to the stockyards."

I can think of worse neighbourhoods at that, and am the more amazed in that these are Irish folk (two generations back), whose grandparents probably shared their roof trees with the small cows of Kerry which gave them butter for their bread.

This pasture, by the way, is the piece of wild land already mentioned as the home of the merlins and the badgers, and in which lies the old Indian camping ground with its rings of stones.

Next to the lake is a large grove of Manitoba maples, and further east several deep coulees cleave the hillside, and also hold maple trees of this small species. They grow wide, with short main trunks and long, crooked limbs so close to the ground that on the steep places many of the uphill ones actually rest their elbows on the bank. We can see the healed auger holes made by Indians in years past to tap the trees and release the flow of April sap from which they made their tasty sugar cakes.

Tallest of the trees are the elms, which stand with limbs upthrust in every attitude of abandon. In contrast with these wild witch trees, the ashes—so evenly developed—look positively prim.

The pasture is a favourite place for jack rabbits, and we often surprise one from his form. Their narrow trails show up quite plainly in the grass, and run as straight as survey lines up hill and down, with little of that regard for topography which is shown by the trails of moose, deer, or cattle.

Once, in the grass, we found a litter of young jacks, all cosily tucked up in a nest of mother hare's downy fur. There they crouched, ears tight to their napes, eyes open and unblinking, while the wind—fleet as their grey mother—caressed their soft fur. So we left them, and saw Old Wat hopping hesitantly in the grass, showing herself to lure us away, risking death to protect her young.

The wind is almost constant here at the crest of the hill. Sometimes it roars in from the northwest, sending the white horses galloping down the lake in endless procession, till they break their knees on the shoreside rocks and dissolve in froth.

At such times the lake can be dangerous, and every year there are accidents of some kind. Once, in a sudden storm, we stood anxiously at the window for over an hour, peering through field glasses at a tiny dot of a boat on the far side of the lake. The owner had been fishing near the Arm River Bridge on a still morning when, noticing the rising wind, he pulled anchor and started north, toward his cottage. The wind was west-nor'west. Very cautiously he proceeded, gradually cutting down his motor as the wind increased, until he was moving very slowly. We could see him plainly, hugging the west bank as closely as hidden rocks would allow. As each rolling wave approached, he tacked sufficiently to avoid a sideways blow (which would have swamped him) and then brought his craft back into the right direction. This he repeated time and again with the utmost skill till he was directly opposite his dwelling. Then, between waves, he opened his engine and tore for the little wharf upon which his anxious family waited.

We rarely see a rowboat or a canoe on our lake now, such as I remember on my occasional visits of forty years ago. Everyone has a speedboat, and the arts of paddling and rowing are well-nigh forgotten—although the modern craft is obliged to carry one or other of the instruments for hand propulsion in case of engine failure. These boats are built bigger (and therefore better?) each year, and appear to be more highly varnished and equipped with more new gadgets. Undoubtedly they are a great joy to their owners, who will talk considerably about them, pointing out their more important features.

One of our friends took us for a boat ride to Regina Beach, several miles across the lake. The trip occupied only seven minutes, and we had a fine view of dashing spray—but little else—to the accompaniment of a strong smell of oil and an ear-splitting roar.

Regina Beach was the first of many beaches on this lake to be used by summer campers and later by cottagers. It is now a large village. Before cars were in common use a daily train plied back and forth from the city to serve the beach lovers.

Along this beach is still to be seen one of the last of the grain barges, long fallen into disuse. In the period before the extension of the branch railroad to the north end of the lake, the Pearson Land Company undertook to form a navigation branch to run a passenger and freight service on the sixty-mile stretch of water. In some respects Last Mountain Lake more nearly resembles a wide river or fjord, for in spite of its length it is only a few miles wide at the most. Indeed, one Welsh-born friend of mine who often comes for a weekend tells me that, seen from the cottage, the lake resembles nothing so much as a view of the waters of Milford Haven.

At all events, this old grain barge with its fellows once plied the length of the lake, loading bagged grain at the various ports of call, of which the closest (to us) were Glen Harbour, a few miles north; Regina Beach, across to the south; and Valeport (the end of navigation) at the southeastern extremity.

Passengers for the north were taken uplake by the steamer *Qu'Appelle,* which was, from all accounts, a beautiful craft. I have only seen old photographs of her, but these show her graceful lines and the luxury of her interior.

Besides bona fide travellers, the northward trip attracted many of the upper crust of Regina society, who went for the outing and the good meals in the dining saloon. The gay music and the jolly company must have been a great treat and a real pleasure to dwellers in the Queen City, and a nostalgic experience for the many English men and women who had once made similar excursions on the Thames. But with the coming of the railway this phase of transportation quietly folded up, and it is now only a happy memory to the older generation.

There is still a yacht club at Regina Beach, but it is only rarely that we see one of these graceful craft pass by. There is not, perhaps, much pleasure in sailing in close proximity to the noise and heavy wash of the speeding, ever-circling turbo-jets which wake the echoes and the gulls. Yachting is an occupation for more leisurely, contemplative men—who should smoke a pipe. The only common reminder of this hobby is to be seen in the white yachting caps still worn rather incongruously by speedboat enthusiasts.

But, surprisingly, many of the personnel of the Royal Canadian Navy are prairie boys, and not a few of them first made contact with the water on Last Mountain Lake.

Commercial fishing is still carried on in winter, but not at the south end of the lake—that is reserved for angling. One of the favourite angling spots is near the Arm River Railway Bridge already mentioned. This is crossed by the line from Regina Beach up the west side of the lake, and it is situated at the very mouth of the Little Arm, as this locality is commonly called.

The river takes its rise some forty to fifty miles north and west, its birth waters formed by two springs which lie in a coulee draining most of the high, rolling country of the Allen Hills. Just as the Silton area is spoken of as "bluffy country" and the flat, treeless area is called "the plains," so the broken country around the head of Arm River is popularly called "the hills."

The ranches there have a lovely location—the green, lush meadows, the big godwits flying about, the winding creek all over-hung with willows, the sage-sweet, sloping hills dotted with black cattle and horses of every colour—black, bay, buckskin, and grey, with flashy pintos and sorrels.

The Anglo-Saxons are a modest people, not given to much talk, and I sometimes think that the many in the West are not too well understood for that reason. They love everybody but themselves, it seems, and seek no recognition. Even the mass media hardly recognise them (except for an occasional barked or affected "English" voice); and when it presents Bonnie Scotland in song and verse the Saxons listen with a rising pulse, as they do with tautened heartstrings (and something like guilt) to the music of the Distressful Country. Their throats contract as the voices of St. David's land transport them from the living room to realms of Cromlechs and Druids. The songs of the Ukraine stir them, as the wind stirs the grasses and grain on our wide, new steppes.

But seldom do they hear the praises of the land of Wordsworth and the Woolsack, of Maypoles and Milton—the voices which speak for the spirit, the wealth, the happiness, and the conscience of England. And then the fare is thin and meagre, like "skilly" after puddings and pies, and the reaction is apt to be the self-conscious ejaculation: "I say, steady on!" which might sound casual, if not derogatory; but it is the highest praise from a race noted for understatement, whose hearts are strangers to their sleeves.

The Anglo-Saxons are notoriously slow and self-contained.[5] And yet—as the controversy over Canada's new flag has shown—they have a mind and a will, and can be extraordinarily tenacious. They will forgive an enemy, a slight or an insult. They give gen-erously, but balk at being robbed. The leaders of our country have not always been aware of this quiet sense of purpose, perhaps misunderstanding respect for law and order, and judging it to be indifference.

These people have contributed very greatly to the moulding of the frontier, in an unassuming way; for they brought poetry and painting, pianos and puddings, and many more things which are "requisite and necessary as well for the body as the soul." The works of Milton and Shakespeare, the Bible, as well as fine china and chintz, and loyalty to the Crown—and a strong objection to any attack on those ancient and time-honoured institutions which they protected so stubbornly against their Norman overlords in bygone days.

Essentially a rural people, they have not perhaps excelled in the world of business and commerce; nevertheless, they have more surely brought *civilisation* than have any railroads, fine buildings, or other developments which are popularly supposed to be the forerunners of that happy state. Civilisation is carried in the spirit rather than in the pocketbook, and the civilised man takes it with him.

I do not agree with those who say that the Englishman, by virtue of his love of things English, by his nostalgic regard for tradition, cannot or does not make a "good Canadian." Is a man a better husband for forgetting the precepts of his mother? If England is the mother of the English Canadian, Canada is his wife and the mother of his children. God forbid there should be a clash of loyalties! If, in building the new, the Saxon wishes to retain the best of the past, may he not hang his grandfather's picture in his wife's sitting room? To say he may not, does not denote a more fervent Canadian patriotism; rather, it is a sign of immaturity.

It has been said that English Canada "holds back" Canadian unity. I am not referring here to what our French Canadian compatriots call "English Canada"—which (except for language) is not English at all, for it makes no distinction between Jew and Gentile, as it were. When Quebec gets impatient with the English, she is apt to blame England, the country; yet (and this is not meant to be even a suggestion of criticism) the voice of "English" Canada is more Celtic than Saxon.

The Scot is attracted to figures, to matters fiscal, political, and inventive, and is perhaps at his best in the Board Room. But your Saxon is only truly himself at his books or in the rural atmosphere of his garden.

He will only become a leader when his patience is exhausted; and perhaps, too, when the voices of the ultra-nationalistic have died down a bit, and people stop worrying so much about a "national" culture. In the meantime, he is a good whipping boy. If his "Empire" has broken down, he will not forever—as his accusers may think—sink into despair. His so-called "aristocratic vision" can be modified to fit our new nationalism, without any loss of his ideals.

My own "nostalgic" writings do not mean that because my father is dead I am in despair; far from it. The challenge of today awaits.

The Saxons are, perhaps, the least brilliant of our ethnic groups, but if the flowers of Canada blossom under the hands of Celts and Slavs and Norsemen; if the savour of her sap, her élan, and her warm devotion to God are of France; the sturdy heartwood of her trunk is still largely composed of English oak.

"If I forget thee, O Jerusalem, may my right hand forget her cunning" is not a groan of despair, but rather a shout of ecstasy.

Our Canadian growth may be a hybrid tree, but she is not barren; her flowers will set, her fruit mature.

Consider now how August ripens, and the crop—already feeling the sickle—awaits our greater labours.

CHAPTER VI

September—The Moon of Bread

The long Labour Day weekend is a time for celebration at the lake cottages. The hardtop road from Regina is crowded with cars at the City end, but gradually the ranks thin out as the cottagers for Regina Beach, Lumsden Beach, and Saskatchewan Beach take their respective side roads.

The lakeside at Pelican Point, which has slumbered in the dusk for a week, bursts into blossom on Friday night. You hear voices, the slamming of doors; commands to children: "Shut the door! The fish flies are coming in!" And one by one the porch lights are snapped on and send their beams reaching up the hillside, casting weird shadows on the steep grass slope behind us as we go and come.

For there must be light. The country is inhospitable when darkness sets in, at least for people unaccustomed to adjusting their eyes to the light of stars, and little feet may stumble between the cottage and the "biffy."

On the morrow there will be water sports for the gregarious—the speedboats will dart hither and thither, water skiers following in their wake; drawn, it would seem, invisibly, for from our distance you cannot see the connecting rope.

For the more solitary, there is fishing.

"Labour Day" has a nice sound. But it means little now; for who understands labour—sweet labour—which is man's curse and blessing? We avoid it, and the Seven Deadly Sins tell us it is brutalising.

The farmers see little of this, and care less. Certainly some of the well-to-do among them also have cottages, but these are for the children and the wives now; for the harvest is in full swing, and daily the acres of standing grain dwindle, and the fields become zebra-striped with the swaths which flow around from the edge to the centre, lying like snakes along the curvatures of the golden stubble, over the swells and across the hollows.

There are few stooks nowadays—few of those serried rows of little golden tipis, accommodating themselves to the self-supporting cone shape found in all primitive plains dwellings where there is no natural support and where the wind runs riot.

People still like pictures of fields of stooks, but the artist now must travel far to find such a subject for his brush. But this is another example of how we cling, culturally, to outworn symbols. The stook was the symbol of bread—but we eat little bread today compared with formerly. In earlier days, when we worked harder and had fewer luxuries, a hungry stooker or thresher ate his loaf a day, and the prairie housewives made big loaves and baked twice a week.

The stooks used to provide sunning places for the prairie chickens who came to glean the field. We would be early at our work of stooking the bundles left in rows by the clattering binder, and in these early hours we would see the birds, statuesque on the stook tops, dark against the molten rays of the rising sun. At the sound of our voices, and the brittle crackling of the stubble beneath our heavy boots, they would fly clucking to the nearest bluff or patch of shrubbery.

These have gone—almost. Very rarely we see a small covey. We miss them.

The stook was a miniature Coat of Arms for the acres of plenty, and the prairie chickens the surmounting Crest. The Motto might well have been: *"Keep up to the Binder!"*—for this was the good stooker's pride.

Harvesting today is a lonely job. Where once it engaged many hands, we now see a solitary man perched high on a painted, shuddering Juggernaut. If the wind is cold and the day cloudy, he is muffled to the eyes against those elements. We see the Great Machine and its tiny operator top the crest of the swells and disappear in the hollows, only to reappear, with an inevitable monotony. Against the slanting beams of the evening sun there is a beauty in the inexorable monster with its dinosaur-like head, swimming, as it were, through its golden cloud of shattered straw and husks.

But there is something sad, too, in the dust-laden figure on its lofty perch; a man condemned to everlasting dedication to a weary journey, which starts at a field corner and goes on and on, round and round, day and night. For long after darkness falls on the land the work goes on, and from a hilltop you can see the lights of combines flashing—now here, now there—and a steady moan fills the land.

How different from our earlier conception of a harvest scene! The old British landscape painters have left us priceless treasures of what harvesting once meant. Here is the rolling cornland. The spire of the village church is seen, peering above the nodding wheat heads (for the church is in the vale). The reapers, red handkerchiefs at neck, follow each other in perfect rhythm—you can see they are singing. Then the stookers plant the new-bound sheaves upright, pushing the butts well into the stubble. A couple, their turn for lunching having come, sit in the shade of some rustling sheaves. One holds his bread in hand, keeping the slices of cheese in position with his calloused, useful thumb; the other pushes back a few bearded wheat heads which are tickling his ear.

The girls are there, too—some bringing baskets of lunch, and we know there will be mild, sweet onions and boiled bacon, as well as the cheese. Coats lie under a bush, and a faithful dog keeps guard.

There is light, colour, and song in this scene. This is fulfillment.

Today we don't hear the swish of scythes or the snatches of song. We don't even hear the clatter of yesterday's binder, which had a merry sound, nor the cheery commands to the straining horses: *"Whoa! Gee!* Har over—*Lady!"* All we hear is the moaning of the dinosaur.

Yet, is this really Harvest? Or is it only, as they now say, "taking off the crop"—like that?

If it is Harvest, where is the voice—the spirit—of full-blown Summer?

Do we hear it in the meshing of gears, or the explosions—so many hundreds a minute—as it was heard from the throats of bearded reapers, working with gowns tucked up to their waists? As it was heard in the whetting of scythes in the barley fields of Boaz? As it floated—wind-blown—from the brittle stubble, crushed by the bare feet of Ruth? Does its song rise as it did in the dusk of the threshing floor, while the unmuzzled oxen trampled the yielding straw?

Nobody sings any more. We do not hear the songs of England, of Scotland, of Germany or the Ukraine—or Zion. Once these people sang at their work, their voices lilting over the flatlands, rising upward from the glens. Is it that we now live in a "strange land?" Is it because of radio and TV that we have become receivers only—never giving? Never sending forth our spirit upon the morning air? When we lost the art of song, was it because our spirit broke when farming became a business instead of a craft?

But I have forgotten.

The Indians still sing. You can hear them sometimes if you drive at dusk over the dim trails which slide and crawl across their Reserve. You will hear the soft plunk of a drum, and then—if you take time to stop your car—the ancient chanting song will creep into your ear, into your bloodstream, carrying you back to ancestral dusks. Now high, now in trembling decline, the notes hang beneath the stars; and you know, somehow, that these songs are set to dim and obscure beginnings.

Also, the grasshoppers sing—not at all like a melancholy hurdy-gurdy as Longfellow says, for their music is vibrant and full of life. It is like the whetting of many scythes or reaping hooks —those semicircular blades which unite with man's arm for the gathering in of his bread.

I wonder what we have lost?[1] I grope for it, but it eludes me. Is it something half-real, half-fancied? Something which, like my blood, goes back to the beginning of things? A lost Golden Age, perhaps, that has persisted only in dreams?

Whatever it is, it tells me that slowly, inexorably, we lose the Art of Life. We surrender the muses as hostages to the invading forces of technocracy.

Have we become only a swarm of bees, to be counted by hives? Robbed of our honey, and fed instead on the soothing syrup of security? As if there was no death, no ancient Reaper of Man to know us individually? Or must we die, too, by hives?

But I am wrong. We are not robbed by others; much worse than that. For we push and crowd and elbow into the mass, holding up our money, begging to purchase our own undoing.

Long ago in old Greece a wise man said: "The gates of excellence are surrounded by a sea of sweat." Today's harvest field reeks not of sweat, but of gasoline or diesel fuel.

I am afraid this applies in many other fields, too. How much we miss by using today's swift transportation! In this, the artist and the naturalist make a mistake—for we think the world is smaller. We think there is a more interesting bird, a more sublime view, a more picturesque nook, beyond the hills; and we speed unheeding past a thousand unseen creatures, past unnoticed views, neglected nooks and crannies. No artist need take even one step beyond where he stands to find a subject for his brush. We long to see the mountains; or course, they are lovely—but why sigh for them when the hillside is bathed in gold?

We walk, Hope and I, as often as we ride. We may see more in half a mile than in fifty miles on the hardtop; and, after all, it is what one sees, not the number of miles travelled, that makes a journey memorable. The sweat is incidental, and not unpleasant.

One day we went by bus to Regina.

I don't drive in the city; too much time is wasted finding parking space. So we drove to Craven, the next town—for the highway upon which the bus travels, bypasses Silton, but stops at a store in Craven to pick up passengers.

This bus we like. We like being free of responsibility, and we like the courteous, friendly driver—the natural heir and successor to the stagecoach drivers of an earlier day. These men carry responsibility with a smile, and theirs is a craft—to know the condition of the road by the look of it, to put their great tires on the least icy places, as we once reined our teams so that they might find footing for their clever hooves.

We left the car with the friendly storekeeper, and now the bus crossed the lovely valley of the Qu'Appelle—that much-painted valley that is seen on the canvases of Henderson and Kenderdine and dozens more. And we climbed the long hill through the gilded September groves, and crossed the great level Regina plain, where we left all the groves behind and could see the dim outline of elevators many miles away and the slow-moving combines, each with its dust cloud. There are no fences here, and the road cuts through one endless chessboard of squares—the dull orange of wheat, the yellow of mustard, and the brown of summer fallow.

The tires sing as we rush ever onward towards the pools of water which glisten on the blacktop, but as we approach the pools dry up, for they are not blue water at all, but pools of light reflected from the dark surface of the road; mirages in miniature, like those seen by thirsty travellers in the Sahara. And as disappointing, for we were sure we would hear the splash and see the spray fly up to wet the windshield.

Coming back from Craven we see dim, dark forms crowding the P.F.R.A. pasture at Valeport, and we stop our car to look. But they are bales of hay, not cattle. Later, when the lush aftermath is high enough, there will be grazing beasts to feed on it.

Each morning we hear the hollow voices of swans, the insistent, strident gabbling of geese, and the tinny notes of cranes.

Swans fly purposefully, dark against the morning sky, necks outthrust, wings beating steadily, never sailing like pelicans; or they settle quietly on the water, their mass glistening like a great ice raft far from shore, pure white amidst the blue-green water.

The lines of geese, by comparison, seem desultory, rising and falling as their notes swell and diminish.

But the cranes are circling high, spying out a landing place, mere dots against the blue, a little plainer when below a white cloud. They weave in a never-ending pattern, the tail-enders eventually intermingling with the fore-flyers. They will probably settle at the north end of the lake, on those same parched levels on which we were caught by the July thunderstorm. This is perhaps the greatest gathering ground for sand-hill cranes in all of Canada. Like flocks of range turkeys, they stalk far and wide in pursuit of grasshoppers—which abound on these grasslands. The herbs and low shrubbery conceal the length of their legs, and no wonder the country people call them *wild* turkeys. Later, they will flock out at earliest daybreak to feed on the grain fields.

Up to now, these lovely birds have been protected by the "Migratory Birds Treaty Act," but there have been complaints of damage, and this year the authorities have been persuaded to declare an open season, with the hope that shooting will cause the birds to scatter. The farmers and tourists see so many thousands of cranes that they are led to believe that they are a common bird and a pest; but actually this is not a true picture, for nearly all the cranes of North America are gathered here annually. This is their traditional halfway resting place between their nesting grounds on the Arctic tundra and their winter home within call of the Gulf States. The birds we saw last winter on the Chihuahua Desert had themselves dropped down at Last Mountain Lake the previous autumn. The Mexicans call them *campesinos*—countrymen—and, indeed, in the far golden haze they look like wayfarers. My son tells me that in the far northwest of Australia another crane is called "native companion" by the Blackfellows.

Cranes, *campesinos,* companions, turkeys—by whatever name, these noble birds have long been associated with the arts of man. Jeremiah tells us: "Yea, the turtle and the crane . . . observe the time of their coming." *Agur* (in Latin, *grus*), the twitterer, the

Hebrews called this bird, although to us his call sounds more like a rattling. The tall artifacts of iron which hung in the chimneys of early England, from which were suspended the pots and pans, were called "cranes." We see these birds depicted in a dozen poses among the lotus reeds on Egyptian bas-reliefs, and the Japanese have traced and coloured them in all their graceful beauty on many a sheet of rice paper.

We hope we can keep our cranes, but it is doubtful.

True, a large part of the north-end lowlands is officially called a game preserve, but that title means little today. Like the parks, such areas are used more and more by people, the deadliest enemies of wildlife.

Recreation areas would be a better description; but for the sake of groups of people interested in the protection of our flora and fauna—like the Saskatchewan Natural History Society—the other term is used. It forestalls in advance any complaints that such societies may make. So those responsible (or irresponsible) for "wildlife management" have developed a whole vocabulary to camouflage their actions. "Parks" and "Reserves" are some of the terms hiding development of quiet areas into public recreation (and nuisance) grounds, with their golf courses, camping and eating facilities, boating, and all the rest.

In the garden, our self-seeded wild sunflowers nod and tremble all day to the onslaughts of the goldfinches who feed on the now-maturing heads. They are a little family group. The paterfamilias is as yellow as the flowers, showing black only on wingtips, tail, and forehead. The mother is a more sober reflection, though yellow indeed, and not as nut-brown as the children. *Pick-a-seed,* they keep saying, and bend downward over the swaying seed heads to pull out a sweet kernel in their hurried way—for they keep a sharp lookout, and if we slam the screen door they scatter in quick flight, still saying *pick-a-seed, swee-eet?*

Once a lone crossbill came too, but he (or she) was tamer, and fed more deliberately. We could not tell its sex, for it was an immature bird of a species called the red crossbill. They are unpredictable birds—now here, now there—and, for all they are credited with a breeding range in the northern coniferous forest, this one may have been hatched in one of the spruce shelter belts in the vicinity. He—it—stayed for days and paid no heed to us. Hope was intrigued with its crossed bill, which looks so awkward and is yet such a perfect tool for the opening of pine cones or poplar galls.

The early Christians said that this little bird attempted to remove the nails from the crucified Christ, but only succeeded in putting its bill out of shape. They said, too, that the red breast worn by the male is in remembrance of the blood which flowed from Christ's hands. We don't put stock in such stories nowadays, but in the evergreen forests of the Carpathians and of Germany the mothers still tell them to the children.

Sandpipers, birds of the year, nurtured on Arctic shores, are still arriving, and the Point is possessed by little flocks of many species, as well as by sanderlings, tripping among the large gulls, or flying in little groups along the shore.

We know badgers are about, for you can see their scuts, dry and crumbly. If you look closely you know they have been feeding on crickets and grasshoppers, for here are the desiccated wings, round heads, and legs as rough as files.

One night we went down to the maple grove and sat on an uprooted tree. The moon was high, but hiding a little behind the interlaced arabesques of terminal twigs, as shy birds love to do. The night was full of sound—crickets clicking their castanets, grasshoppers shrilling from the hillsides, where grassy slopes still held the warmth of the September day.

Then came a thudding and a scattering of newly fallen leaves, and there in the moonlight was a badger—Old Brock himself. He sat like a bear and snuffed at the strange human scent. We sat as still as mice. We saw the moonlight on his hoary doormat of a coat, the white stripes on his muzzle and up between his short ears. More rustling, and his mate appeared. And then, one by one, the cubs, three in number, already grown half as large as their elders.

All snuffed in turn, before scattering noisily to resume their search for the cocoons, the tender roots, and the beetles for which they were foraging.

Their den, we knew, was far up the hillside. We had seen the freshly displaced earth, and the other signs about its mouth which proved its occupancy. But I believe that only we of all the cottage dwellers ever saw the badgers themselves, or cared to.

From the cottage windows the lights beamed forth, and we heard the tinny thumpings of television sets. Perhaps they showed a family of badgers on the screen that night? But they would be ghosts only, and even Walt Disney films cannot reproduce the soft night breeze on your cheek, nor the smell of newly fallen leaves, nor the sweet-sour perfume of bush cranberries in the coulee.

The elevator works full blast in September and even then it bulges at the seams, and you can see great piles of wheat in the fields, confined within a circle of hay bales. They are heaped to a perfect cone, and will run off the heaviest rain. But cattle must not be allowed to stray; for should they plunder the piles by night, the dawn will show one or more animals lying dead from bloat, their stiff legs sticking up indecently from their swollen bodies.

The train clanks north pulling an unbelievable length of empty cars behind the diesel engines, which look mere pygmies compared to the great steam locomotives we remember. The cars are destined for northern points, and will return later on, brimful of wheat.

There are two railway lines hereabouts—the one passing up the west side of the lake, visible from our cottage, and the other up the east side, which goes through Silton and Lanigan. The one on the west side goes to Colonsay to meet the east-west main line of the Canadian National. From the cottage we hear this train rumble across the Arm River Bridge, and then see it slowly crawling up the far shore. There is a road crossing directly opposite the cottage, and at this the train whistles; we know it is almost dinner-time, and we wave, but the engineer would need a good telescope to see us.

When I was a boy we had what we called the potato train at Robertsbridge. It came down the narrow-gauge, and passed the villages at eleven-forty, and it warned the village women to put the spuds to boil for their men's dinner.

The shooting season is on us, and from all sides we hear the dull reports of shotguns in twin bursts of sound. Shotgun fire does not roll and reverberate like the barking of rifles.

The Little Hungarian partridges must be more cautious now. As we drive to and from town we notice the dwindling numbers within the coveys we have seen grow up from downy chicks to full-sized targets, coveys which have fed along their chosen parts of the roadside, converting weed seeds to muscle and sinew and feathers. Where a family group contained perhaps fifteen members, we now see them gradually reduced to ten—to six— perhaps to one lone bird who calls *caa-rack—caa-rack?* in the gloaming, but is not answered.

We often pass dead porcupines on the roads. These poor creatures, now flattened by truck wheels and picked at by scaveng-ing crows, are night feeders and night travellers, and it is while they attempt to cross the road after dark that the dazzling car lights are their undoing. One lovely September night I saw some-thing moving ahead on the Pelican Point hill. I was able to slow up, and beheld that rare sight, a stout mother porcupine conducting her five young for their evening walk. The young ones were about the size of half-grown rabbits, and their hair (rather than fur) was the colour of ripening oats—still greenish, but warmly tinted with ochre and yellow. Their quills had not yet grown long enough to be visible among the long, coarse hairs, but I well knew that those wicked spear points lurked like pin feathers beneath their jackets. They all stood and stared; the mother, and behind her the Indian file of her children. I had to put out my lights and wait a few minutes for them to decamp, and not till I heard the pattering of their feet in the trash of the ditch did I venture forward once more.

Sad to say, the roadsides are death traps to many creatures. First, there is the hazard of the motor vehicles, and most of the shattered bodies in the dust are victims of the crushing wheels, or—in the case of birds—of the windshields. Then again, many hundreds of birds—especially Hungarian partridges and prairie chickens—meet their death by collision with the telephone wires; I see three or four on every short journey, varying from the sora rails to blackbirds, upland plovers and nighthawks. Birds which are slower and more desultory of flight are seldom victims of this danger, and I have yet to find a magpie or a buzzard hawk thus killed; though I once picked up a sharp-shinned hawk, who had been presumably in full cry after some small bird.

The ground squirrels (gophers) must also beware of the road, especially in September, when the grain spilled from the brimming trucks is a strong attraction. Not only may the cars crush them, but the big buzzard hawks—especially the Swainson's and red-tailed—choose to perch on the telephone poles for hours, and they will pounce down on any gopher who dares appear in the open. By night, it is owls which take their place. Horned owls are looking for road-crossing rabbits, but the short and long-eared kinds make war mostly on mice.

Every year a pair of ferruginous hawks—of the rough-legged group—nest somewhere near Silton, but try as I will I cannot locate their eyrie, although in my search I have found numerous nests of horned owls and buzzards. These birds are uncommon so far north and east, for their more favoured habitat is the high plains of the Coteau, where in the absence of trees they build their great nests on the buttes. Perhaps my Silton birds have a private cutbank near the lake. All I know is that each fall I see them hunting, and against the summer fallow they look very light, for—as their name indicates—they are rust-coloured, and as they flap in pursuit of grasshoppers they show the white or pale fawn of their underwings.

But if the roads are death traps to some, there are still many species which first saw the world in the dust and glare, for along the fenceline we see perched the kingbirds and the shrikes, the vesper sparrows, the bluebirds and the sparrow hawks, whose nests are not far distant.

Cattle are crowding the stubble lands. They are the gleaners today, for we need not be thrifty with our wheat, and they wander at will through the dying and brittle stalks.

The poplar bluffs are gold in the sunshine, russet and purple in the shade. The September haze turns the far hills to blue, and the horizon is lost.

Already some leaves are fallen, and the Russian thistle by the roadside changes colour with the first frosts from dull olive and terre verte (earth green, an artist's colour) to rich umber, to red, giving new colour where lately the purple asters and the goldenrod flaunted their multiple shades.

The beauty is there, rather added to than robbed by the changes, the maturing, just as a woman's golden hair is the more lovely for that gleam of silver which must crown her glory.

September now is dying.

She is feminine, this lovely gentle month. She has brought forth in abundance. Many of the crops will yield thirty to forty bushels per acre of good amber wheat for England, for China, for us.

But September must die from the effort, and masculine October will soon stride across the prairie with an eye for the North.

But look! As the leaves fall, the buds are on the naked twigs!

CHAPTER VII

October—The Moon of Spirits

Hardly has September flashed her last smile than October comes in, accompanied by cold rain and a bone-chilling wind from the northeast.

We are weather-conscious in the country. We need to be, for the nature of our daily work depends upon the skies, the temperature, and the wind.

City folk must find us irritating at times, for even when we pay them a visit we are bound to look up at the sky, or out of the window, and ask continually: "Did you get the weather report?" But they didn't, and shake their heads; for office workers must follow the same routine day after day, and in the short trip between home and office they remain snugly sheltered with little regard for the vagaries of the natural world.

Imagine the office manager of a company having to say: "Girls, we can't do any filing today—it's too windy!" They pay as little heed to the weather as to the sounds around, for the sounds of commerce have no such significance as a sudden gust in the barnyard, the spatter of an over-boiling stew pot, or the high-pitched voice of a lost calf.

Artists, poets, surveyors, explorers, and priests, no less than farmers, enjoy the constantly changing scenes, the variety of tasks which—unless they are victims of a slave complex—give them the peace and happiness which make "vacations" unnecessary. Which, to borrow from Ruskin's remarks on the weather, means there are no such things as "nice jobs" or "nasty jobs"—only different kinds of "pleasant jobs."

The last leaves are falling, dropping silently in the rain, their early crispness wilted. The bluffs and the clumps are left as grey and obscure as twilight, for the autumn rain is now cooling the earth, and the mists of morning shroud every scene.

Even after the sky has cleared, which it presently does, we find little colour left in the landscape. The grey trees blend softly with the greying stubble, the browsing deer themselves are hardly distinguishable until they move, or with white banner held high dash for cover. Here and there, it is true, a few wine or russet leaves still hang, or a patch of roseberries adds a note of sealing-wax red.

Only the skyscape is as vivid as ever—perhaps more so by contrast with the sheared and denuded land. The sunsets make you catch your breath as, for brief moments, the sun in the pause before his final plunge regilds the hills with the colours of September; but when he leaves us the greyness descends again, only the brief seconds of the afterglow reviving for a moment a pale shadow of remembered glories.

The air grows chilly.

It will freeze tonight, and the tinkling flocks of pipits which lately walked the summer fallow are silent. We have had our fall rain, and the clear sky and dropping temperature by night foreshadow the mellow reign of Indian summer.

Plato, Buddha, Moses—the great congregation of prophets and leaders of the ancient world—were all believers in thankfulness and rejoicing, and their thoughts have been knit into our civilisation. As the heavenly bodies are to the sun—not beaming forth light themselves, but acting as mirrors—so did these great souls reflect the light of Christ, who was to come, yet had been before all ages.

Thankfulness.

Harvest Thanksgiving is an old, old custom, and still we have a Service in the village Church in its honour. If the traditional offering of thanks to Him who "gave and preserved to our use the kindly fruits of the earth so as we may in due time enjoy them" has now been mixed up with the Thanksgiving dinner of the Pilgrim Fathers, it is nevertheless good; so long as we remember that our ploughing and scattering of the good seed has been blessed. Isaac Walton, that redoubtable and compleat angler, said that a thankful heart is one of the dwelling places of God. *"Or any ill escaped or good attained,"* wrote Shakespeare, *"let us remember still Heaven chalked the way that brought us thither."*

Henry Ward Beecher puts it another way: *"The unthankful heart . . . discovers no mercies."*

Hope loves to walk down the hill and to the end of the point of an evening. There she stands, or sits on a rock, and notices the birds, or just gazes across the water.

She hears the splashing of coots, the sound of ducks flying overhead in the quiet dusk after the guns are silent for the day; she hears the western grebes call from the gloom far across the water. Sometimes she sees a heron or a muskrat, and once a group of Bonaparte gulls. On her return, if I have not been with her, she tells me all she saw in short, almost breathless sentences— for sometimes she comes back running, with thoughts of supper to cook.

Sometimes she prefers to climb to the uplands, following the edge of a gullied coulee splitting the hillside; what a friend of ours called "a hairy armpit," in contrast to the rounded shoulders of the ascent.

The hills by the lake seem to flow downward from the prairie level in undulations. The changes of angle are not abrupt—they are like the pauses that one sees in the languorous yet compelling dances of Spain. They do not shock, as a cliff shocks, but rather seduce us further, whether upward or downward.

The rolling prairies above have a smooth, down-like quality, and the higher knolls rise as placidly from the plain as the humped backs of whales basking in a golden sea.

Ruffed grouse can be seen on these October nights as they

perch, roosting, on the crooked wide-branched elms outlined
against the sky.

The bush cranberries smell rankly in the darkness. Their scent
is like the scent of a fox; and, indeed, a fox following his nose
may pick a few with delicately curled lip, to sweeten his supper
of mice and crickets.

Indian summer is here, the rain clouds gone and the air
sweet with smoke from burning brush piles, filling the air with
haze, as the smoke from the peace pipes filled the council lodges
of the feathered chiefs of long ago.

Soon we shall have to pack up and leave Meadowlark Cottage.
The road plugs full of snow in winter, and already we have seen
the last of our neighbours, who have shuttered their windows and
locked their doors. We would be happy with a horse to take us
back and forth for groceries, but people who object to a few cows
in a pasture would not look kindly on a stable.

The first winter we left in November and went to Mexico,
keeping well away from tourist centres. We found the great dun-
coloured desert of Chihuahua very like our October prairie, with
yellowed grasses replacing our stubble, and bathed in a sun as hot
as ours had been in September.

Last winter we occupied a suite in Regina. We had many gay
evenings with friends, but on the other side of the balance, was
the noisy traffic, the gasoline fumes, the crowds of harassed faces
at the shopping centres, the push, the surge of the anthill. And
in the apartment building there was the thumping of TV sets and
the slamming of doors—a hideous sound to the ears of anyone
brought up in a day when to slam a door was a sin, and you were
sent back to close it properly by turning the handle.

We did not want another winter in the city. We had known the
joy of peace and quiet where no neighbour's smoke could be seen,
no neighbour's dog heard; where the only night sounds had been
the cracking of a log in the frost, the hoot of a horned owl, or
on occasion the solemn chorus of timber wolves.

By the greatest of good luck our storekeeper at Silton had a small house for sale in the village. It was the second dwelling to stand on a foundation of multicoloured prairie stones, built by an old-time mason with the assistance of a brother of the late Jimmy Gardener, who had once been our Provincial Premier.

The house is well built, roomy enough and warm, heated by one of the new oil furnaces which operates by a thermostat. Now, for the first time, we had electricity willy-nilly, but that is in keeping here, as it would not be at the Lake.

The atmosphere of Silton is ideal for our ages and tastes; the people friendly and kind, the distance to the cottage short. We get our mail daily, which is a luxury. At the ranch up north three or four times a year was enough, but our other interests kept us so occupied it did not matter.

We did not want to take furniture from the cottage, so we set about obtaining the necessities. We had neither the money nor the taste for the shiny products of technocracy in the city stores, so we scoured the country attending farm sales, to pick up what we wanted from what other folk had outgrown. At one town, after a sale which had given us an old-fashioned rocking chair, we spent the evening with the parson and his family. We had known them both at Fort Saint John, when he was a missionary parson and the Saskatchewan girl who is now his wife was district nurse.

The house seems to be always full of young girls from six to fourteen; three of these are daughters of the house, the rest are neighbours' children who wander in and out quite casually. Hardly five minutes pass but one or other—or two together—sit to the piano and try out "Chopsticks" or some such piece. On such occasions our parson is apt to shut himself in his study. The little daughter of a neighbour said: "You just ought to hear my mum play!" Just then "Mum" came in for a visit, and we importuned her. After some demur, saying she was out of practice, she sat down at the instrument and began to play "Whispering Pines"—an old piece—and she played it beautifully.

As we sat and listened, I was taken back to the days of my

young innocence; to the day when all women were virtuous and fair, and all men (except villains) brave and strong; when no one had heard of "dope" or "call girls" or "homos" or "beatniks," or the kitchen-sink-cum-gutter despair with which we are now supposed to live; to the days when, far removed from my quiet home in England, I found myself in the Canadian Army and stationed for training in the Saskatchewan town of Moosomin, which nudges the Manitoba border.

Most of us were then too young—and too shy—to have girl friends, so we would go in little groups of chums to the weekly "picture show."

It was the day of the silent film, and the figures on the screen moved in that jerky, hesitating way older people will remember so well.

But we were not without music, for a piano stood below the screen, or a little to one side, and for a couple of dollars a night some young lady—or perhaps an older man—of local talent would follow the shadowy story with an appropriate accompaniment.

We had *The Birth of a Nation,* with marches and extracts from the more popular operas. We had *The Broken Key,* which ran as a long serial. But best of all were the self-contained short plays, and our undivided love belonged to Canada's Mary Pickford.

The accompanist at Moosomin was Miss Ruby Donald, daughter of the postmaster, and there she sat—straight of back, hands poised above the keyboard—watching the screen.

Lights were dimmed, and the show started:

Mary Pickford stands at the ranch gate, chin cradled in plump arms, gazing towards the mountains. Down come Ruby's hands, and the piano responds in dulcet tones, obedient to the soft pedal, with "Whispering Pines."

But what is that? A bearded man, masked and sinister, wearing a (now traditional) black sombrero, has seized the gentle maiden! See? He drags her to his horse, throws her across the saddle. Through the deep pine woods he gallops, and we suddenly recognise him as George Barnes, the original bad man of the screen. The piano is beating out a high, wild, dangerous tune. The gum chewers in the audience work their jaws faster.

The chords become sombre, evil, sneering, as the bad man, having reached the railroad track, gathers the fainting girl in his arms and steps across the ties. We do not understand his fell purpose till he throws her roughly on the rails and binds her into place! As he makes a final adjustment to the horrid gag, which must bruise those tender lips, the sight of an approaching train freezes us to our seats.

The gum chewers' jaws are still in this awful moment. The villain has remounted his horse, and disappeared towards the Black Diamond mine.

Tragedy seems inevitable.

Will the cruel train cut those lovely limbs?

Now, words flash on the screen: *"Help is near!"* A girl sobs quietly somewhere in the darkness behind us. Ruby pauses, then, at the psychological moment launches into "The Charge of the Light Brigade," just as another horseman (Bill Hart) appears. His white woolly chaps proclaim him to be a cowboy. He lashes his blaze-faced mustang with his heavy quirt. Will he be in time? Yes! No! The train slows for the trestle. The cowboy leaves his horse at a bound, is running, gasping. His lips move in prayer. So do ours.

He reaches Mary's side. In a trice she is free, but lifeless (as they used to say for "in a faint"). One arm around her waist, the glossy hair falling like a rivulet—one step and a crouch—and the hero is seen hanging by one hand from the shuddering trestle as the train thunders overhead! I don't remember how he regained that trestle with one arm supporting the girl, but he did—somehow.

Words again flash on the screen: *"Mary, Mary, live for me!"* There is anguish and love in that cry.

He is bringing her around. She opens her eyes. Ruby is playing "The Maiden's Dream."

The father arrives with a hastily gathered posse. (Can that be

Barnes again? Without the mask and the leer?) Why only the father? Because heroines of the Old West cannot have mothers—at least we never see them!

The two men grip hands.

The scene changes, and now the happy lovers stroll hand in hand towards the sunset, which is seen between the tree boles, and once more the sweet strains of "Whispering Pines" fill the drab little building, now transformed, by the alchemy of romance, to the Earthly Paradise.

All this I saw again that night, and I think I shed a tear for something lost.

Remembering other old pieces, I asked the lady if she could play "The Robin's Return." She said she had forgotten, but when Mary discovered the piece in a practice book she found that she had left her glasses behind. In vain did she try first mine, then Hope's; neither pair suited her sight.

So our parson, who had never seen or heard the piece before, essayed it—and did very well, for it is full of fast runs. Hearing it, I remembered how the sister of a friend of mine had pounded out the same tune nearly fifty years ago on a wheezy harmonium in a homestead shack, while outside the snow lay deep all the way to the horizon.

On our way back, we called at the house of other friends. They are farmers, well read, interesting and hospitable. Howard is a great collector of Indian relics and objects of history.

He showed us his neatly labelled collection, housed in the basement—Indian arrowheads, war clubs, stone axes, bone scrapers, and what not. But his fondest treasures he has obtained by digging at the site of old Fort Touchwood, in the hills to the northeast. The fort, one of the later ones here, was built by the Hudson's Bay Company in 1879, and not abandoned till 1909. Here Howard had found various cartridge cases, a bullet mould, pieces of an obviously English teapot which showed a fragment of the Royal Standard in the design, some hand-forged square nails of monstrous size, and a little bottle. Just a common or garden medicine bottle, such as you might buy today, about five inches high. But it was older, even, than yesterday.

Howard's smiling wife gave us a wonderful supper, which featured home-cured ham and real farm bread and butter, and we left as the two sturdy boys, lantern in hand, went to do the barn chores.

As we drove home in the cold October dusk, we talked of the bobcats so many people had seen. And within minutes Hope laid her hand on my arm and said: "Oh, a bobcat! Slow down!"

I slowed. I said: "Where?" She pointed to a telephone pole. We saw the rounded head and feline ears. But it was not a bobcat. It was a great horned owl—a cat that flies.

Our search for furniture was rewarding, and in a week or two we had collected most of our needs. Some old-fashioned chairs, such as Timothy Eaton used to sell when his catalogues catered chiefly to country dwellers. The gate-legged table at which I write. A slightly worn chesterfield. A brass bedstead which nobody wanted, and which fell to me for two dollars; some idiot had painted the brass over with gold paint, now gone dirty rust-coloured, but a little steel wool and elbow grease altered that, and it gleams like new. It is exactly like the bed which was mine as a boy, and is good for a hundred years at least. And, prize of all (for fifty cents!), a couch with real leather cushions, with a barrel churn (crock) thrown in. So do we cast away things of real value, things of personality and craftsmanship. They cannot be handed down to younger people, for the younger people have mostly left the rural areas, and these things won't do in the city—unless you are *very* rich, and a bit eccentric or "arty," and then you can display them as invested snob symbols. (We saw one two-dollar coal-oil lamp go for ten dollars because someone in New York wanted it!)

What lured away the rural people not only from their surroundings but from their happy memories, from their sense of taste and values? What caused their rejection of simple things and the quick donning of sophistication? What was the bait? How was it accomplished?

Mainly by destroying the concept of the dignity of labour, to the end that it should be a forgotten thing; and the young must be dependent on higher education for their living, so as to keep the vast array of educators busy.[1]

As to the dignity of labour, I have seen it in many places. I have in Mexico watched workmen by the hour, amazed at their cheerful acceptance of work. On one occasion some thirty men were pouring concrete. The municipal authorities had engaged to put up a large building with hand labour. The bags of cement and the gravel were unloaded on the pavement, water was hauled with a mule, and the mixing was done with shovels. The carriers used five-gallon petrol cans with wire handles and worked in steady order, the men descending one set of ladders, having their cans filled, and ascending by another ladder, so as to form an endless chain. What struck me was the good humour. The foreman never raised his voice. There was not one ill-natured face; not one indecent or complaining remark; not one exclamation of annoyance. And they toiled under a baking sun, which stood in a sky of Oriental blue.

At noon their women appeared—shawled and heavy-hipped matrons, slim daughters. They set down their baskets of food in the shade, and their men joined them, wiping their brows. They reached their clever, brown Indian hands—so well formed, so sinewy and strong—for the *pan* (the good Mexican loaves), the *tortillas,* enclosing *frijoles refritos,* or perhaps rolled into *burritos* hot with pepper. And oranges, always oranges, the peels of yesterday now dry and spicy in the sun.

So they reached, crossing themselves without haste, not forcing the food at once between their hungry jaws, but savouring it a little letting the first fatigue of the body pass before the final fulfillment. And the women in their black, contrasting with the white cotton of the men, sat too, watching each morsel that their men ate, their own beautiful, useful hands resting also; for they had been to the river that morning to wash on the rocks the clothes their men had soiled yesterday.

Work brutalizing? No, indeed; unless poetry and art, love and duty, are brutal.

A passing American said: "Beats me all how them people are so far behind the times. That could be done with two men and a couple of machines."

He would not have appreciated the fact that these men had honest employment to keep their self-respect. The City Fathers knew. Here was no roar of machinery, no cacophony of harsh sound, no sense of the urgency and haste and bustle which is part of our commercial rat race; just the clip-clop of a mule, the scraping of shovels, the pad of feet on ladders, and a few softly gay or quietly serious words in Spanish.

They were not fighting, not battling nature. They were assisting her at a birth. No sign said that this was the most gigantic, spectacular, tallest, or costliest building in the town. Just some men, dust of dust, using their brother dust and their sister water to mould upward a shelter, a cave aboveground; from the ground, of the ground. And now they were refreshing themselves with the kindly fruits of the earth, brought to their white ranks by the black-garbed women. There is a deep significance in those colours. Women are the vessels of loss—loss of blood when they bear, loss of their menfolk, loss of their years when the tinkling laughter gives way to the cackle of dry lips and toothless gums; and black is the colour of their sorrow. But they wear it with dignity, they would not have it otherwise; for the Latin people of Mexico know the beauty of sadness and the ecstasy which accompanies tragedy, as the Greeks did. They know how to ennoble these things.

And they want their men to wear clean, white cotton—for men are, in a sense, priests; and for these, white unsullied garments are as old as the Ephod of Samuel.

Later, in the warm dusk, a guitar will tinkle. These are no brute beasts. They are happy people.

The first morning we woke up in our new house in Silton, Hope looked at the acres of white walls and started to put up pictures. Then she collected a bunch or two of twigs and red leaves and "weeds" (goatsbeard, sage, wheat stalks), and made the corners bright.

The Indian summer hung on till the end of the month, golden day following golden day, the nights cool and blue, lit by a great moon. On October 24 the temperature at noon was seventy above.

Old fashions survive, but they change their form and are apt to lose their original and inner meaning. So with All Hallows E'en, which we call Halloween. The Irish say that on this day the Devil spits on the blackberries, thus accounting for the mildewed fruit of autumn. The celebrations originated from the pagan feast of the sun's farewell, and it comes at the end of October. Like many pagan feasts—for, as Kipling says, the old gods do not die—this was long ago incorporated into the Christian year, and became the eve of All Saints' Day.

There is precious little significance to the feast now. It has become a frolicking for children, all mixed up with witches, black cats, ghosts, and so forth; actually a return to the pagan Celtic superstitions.

The young people, after the fall of dusk, troop from door to door demanding: "Treats or tricks!" The idea is: "Candies and apples or we'll do you mischief!" So we must placate these threatening hobgoblins and tricksters. Each must have the treats dropped into his or her bag—usually an old pillow slip.

They stand in the doorway masked as pirates, pixies, or even fairies. They do not speak, but stand silent and sinister—walking skeletons, ghosts, witches dismounted—till the honours are done and they troop away, the bigger girls (or are they boys?) leading the tiny ones by the hand. Scarcely has the door closed before another group of young blackmailers arrives; among this lot is a desert-dwelling Arab, and a fairy with a piquant, heart-shaped mask—so perhaps, after all, there are some gentle ones in the half-world of the pixies and leprechauns.

It is innocent fun, and long may it be enjoyed. But the other side, the rank and foolish mischief committed by the bigger youths, is not fun. Actually breaking things, smearing windshields, overturning outhouses, leaving gates open, removing wagon wheels and hiding the axle nuts, docking horses' tails, smearing the udders of milk cows with paint—these are not funny. They are stupid, and they are feeble and cowardly. And the robbing of hen roosts is criminal.

There is little malicious damage at Silton. Some of us had the air let out of our car tires, but a young farmer made the rounds with his pressure pump next day and put all right.

The last goblin vanishes, the last ghost flits away, the last owl hoots, and Halloween is in the past with another October.

CHAPTER VIII

November—The Moon of Frosts

The Indian summer weather held for several days after the turn of the month.

We usually look for "freeze-up" in November, but we can remember unusual years when it came earlier or later. For example, stock grazed out all winter in 1924–25, and we had hardly a cold day and not enough snow for sleighing. Nineteen nineteen was one of the bad ones. It snowed up—deeply—the first week of October, and that snow, with its additions, never thawed until the following April. We threshed with sleighs instead of wagons—combines were not yet in use—and it took a lot of extra hands to loosen and shovel out the snowbound stooks. The twenty-sixth of October that year was fifteen degrees below zero, in contrast to the normal fifty above, or this year's seventy.

It snowed up in much the same way in 1930 after three days of pouring rain, and in this case the storm was accompanied by strong winds, and the drifts were such that there were no trains on the branch lines out of Battleford for several days. One party of west-bound hunters had to spend the night on a local train, and were out of food. However, there followed a big thaw in mid-November, and the remainder of the winter was one of the mildest and most open on record.

The swans remained on the lake till mid-month this year, mostly gathered in a great flock at the southeastern end, by Valeport. From the Lumsden road they were in plain view. The blue water and the background of low, tawny hills made a perfect setting for their wild beauty, while their ululating notes filled the air in contradiction to the name "whistling swan"; for the deep, hollow notes bear no resemblance to such a frivolous sound.

One fine evening, with just enough frost in the air to make it crisp, we drove west of Silton, the swans' voices plain to the ear from our left. What we went to hear, however, was not swans but coyotes. These animals have been so reduced by 1080 poisoning (which is really gassing) that we had not seen a live one for weeks. However, a local farmer told us that he heard them quite often on his place. He had some rough pastureland about a mile north of his buildings, and he thought the little wolves must have denned there. So we drove out on a prairie trail, stopping from time to time to listen. The air was sweet with smoke. A large bluff had recently been bulldozed out, and the pile of trees and scrub, mixed with leaf mould and soil, was burning sluggishly. Every once in a while a tongue of bright flame would shoot upwards, outlining the reeking mass, only to fall back exhausted, for the wood was still green and sappy.

This made a wild, witch-like setting for our anticipated music, which just then started up about a quarter of a mile away.

When a family of coyote pups gives tongue it sounds more like happy, excited laughter than the mournful wail of popular imagination. One says *yap-yap,* and that starts the rest off; they join in with an almost comical chorus of yelps, barks, short howls and whines, often broken off in the middle, but immediately resumed as soon as the choir leader yaps again. The sounds give you no such shivers down the back as do those deep, long-drawn, almost savage roars of timber wolves which shatter the frosty air under the arching lights of the northland.

The 1080 capsules are put out by Conservation Officers, and it seems ironic that these people should be, apparently, much more active in this line of endeavour than in fulfilling the real purposes of conservation—for we never meet with one on protective patrol.

We turned for home, happy to know that at least one pair of

coyotes had escaped a ghastly death and were breeding on the hunting grounds of their ancestors.[1]

We notice, by the car lights, that the bush rabbits are turning white, but it will be a month or more before they are completely snowy. Even then, if you ruffle their fur, you see a bluish tinge below the surface, and this is why the rabbit-skin robes made by the Indians appear so moonlit and silvery. By contrast, the long-legged jack rabbits have fur which is white to the skin.

The weasels, too, are turning, and we met one big fellow head on in the centre of the trail. His eyes gleamed like rubies under our lamps, and we noticed that he was as pied as a pinto horse, part white, part cinnamon brown. When he finally moved it was with an incredible, arrow-like flash of speed. He was probably looking for a rabbit supper, but the bush hares—like the jacks—are scarce this year, and he may have had to be content with mice.

Only once have I been privileged to observe the death dance of a weasel—the antics this animal uses to mesmerize a rabbit. In this he lies and rolls in a sort of ecstasy in full view of his prey, until he has attracted attention. Nearer and nearer he rolls in playful treachery; then, rising, he begins his Salome-like dance, looping, weaving, twining, in all the sinuous beauty of a ballet. But it is a ballet of death, for it ends with a quick leap, a deadly bite at the rabbit's soft nape, and the gurgle of sucked blood.

Remembrance Day, and the mild weather holds. The Veterans are thankful for that. They are not as young as they were when they stepped forward in 1914 and again in 1939, and the cold they once scorned bites into old wounds, brings back old coughs, and stiffens rheumatic legs.

We still have one veteran of South Africa, a handful from the Great War, rather more from Hitler's adventure, together with men who climbed the mountains of Korea.

We are not, perhaps, honoured in the public image today as we were of old. We, who were volunteers for freedom, are now spoken kindly to, and referred to as mere victims of two sides, both wrong. People forget quickly, and are easily indoctrinated by those who, more than anyone else, are chiefly responsible— between wars—for a much greater loss of life than would other- wise be the case[2]; people who have been led to believe that only now (with the Bomb!) are we enlightened; only now have regard for human life; only now at last practise kindness; only now decry racial discrimination.

We sit in a little group—we happy few, we band of brothers— together, in a pew; and we hear the words "Greater love hath no man," and then the Last Post, and in the silence we think of comrades—men perhaps of little learning, but with big hearts and boundless courage—whom we remember as young and eager men, but dead these many years. But they shall never grow old, though our old eyes grow, it might be, a little dim; and we are glad in our hearts, though I am not sure just why. Sorrow and joy are everlastingly intermingled, and perhaps we are glad that, no matter the cost, the job has been done; the dead are at peace, and so are we. Then the choir sings the last hymn, all about the Captains and the Kings and the sacrifice of a humble heart; and their faces shine with a like gladness. They are the mothers, the wives, the daughters, and the aging sweethearts, and they too are at peace in the sure Hope and the everlasting Promise.

The church empties, and the farmers and their families drive back thoughtfully to feed their stock, to eat their supper, and to turn on the radio, which is telling of trouble—trouble in Malaysia, in the Congo, in Cuba, in Mississippi, and in Rhodesia—while the Powers talk of peace.

Not long after this we had a discussion on war toys. The women condemned them, but showed the usual muddled thinking. They compared soldiers to fast-shootin' cowboys,[3] to gangsters, to adult delinquents, and war to unbridled, undisciplined, and ob- jectless street violence. They thought these toys would teach violence and cruelty. They said they tried to teach their children how wrong war was, and these toys taught the opposite! Some thought that cowboy guns were not so bad. None of them seemed to realise that there is such a thing as self-defence, so if Sukarno invades Malaysia . . . ! It makes us old delinquents who tramped through mud and rain to meet the shot and shell wonder whether such people were worth saving from Hitler's breeding programme.

November used to be the great month for hauling wheat to market, and it still is, although with the quota system this job runs through the year. Where we once spent long hours on the road hauling sixty bushels at a time, shoulders hunched to the wind and body tensed against the jolt and jar of wheels, the farmer of today hauls three times that much, and from the cab of his truck cares less about the weather.

One day, about the middle of the month, business took me to Strasbourg, a town twenty miles north. A soft wind was blowing— the tail end of a Chinook that couldn't quite make it east of Moosejaw.

The roads hummed with trucks and cars, for this was the marketing season. Fat cattle—white-faced or polled blacks—surveyed the swiftly passing countryside from the security of the great trucks which rolled south in the dust for Regina. Fast little pickups darted by with sacks of potatoes, a few pigs, or whatever else might be marketable. In town, with sensible disregard for the mild weather, country women trotted in and out of the stores, inspecting winter footwear, feeling woollen goods—for by the calendar winter was just around the corner; and in preparing for the months ahead there must be a nice calculation of the budget.

So much discussion and planning was in progress that scraps of conversation fluttered like butterflies among the prospective buyers: ". . . same as last year, only larger . . . yes, children grow so, don't they?" "Bill ought to be able to get another month's wear out of the old ones, I should think. . . . Then he could start on the new ones at Christmas, and they'll do another fall. . . ." And a man's voice: "Got to get up to the elevator, May! What say I meet you at the Municipal about five?"

I thought: "The West hasn't changed much, after all."

Later I was standing in the Pool elevator. It was just the same as an elevator has always been—and should be. The same crunchy kernels underfoot. The same pigeons sashaying around. The same square of dull autumnal sky seen through the open door. The same lazy trail of smoke smudged across it. The same small group of dusty men by the scales, swapping wheat samples and farming lore.

My mind jumped back fifty years to the old Ogilvie grain elevator at Moosomin. . . . There should be some of the teams coming in from Stanley and Little Bluff and the Pipestone about now. Percherons, gray, dappled, and black, so sleek that you could, as they said, roll an apple from withers to croup, harnessed with Yankee britching that had been brushed by corn tassels in Indiana and Iowa, where they call pigs "hawgs" and stooks "shocks." Great stamping Clydes, white feather swinging to each stride, halting at the soft burr of their owner's command, while the smoke of their nostrils beclouded their tossing heads. You think of the sporrans that swung on the Road to the Isles, and the pause to look back through the mist shroud at Uist and Lewis and Skye; and the broad, craggy, red-headed Canadian sons to whom, in a new land, all these—sporrans and road and islands— have become merely an oft-told tale, a memory misting over, a saga dim with time. Matched teams, these—bays mostly—with wide blazes down their roman noses, chin-whiskered like billy goats, Scotch collar tops with red pompoms bobbing, and brassware winking . . . the high Bain wagons with their sixty-bushel boxes painted green. . . . The teamsters in worn coonskins and tattered fur caps, the stamp of prairie years on their faces, the cud of MacDonald's Chewing tucked into their lean cheeks. . . .

Across the track, from within the snug sanctuary of the Huron Hotel, the Ancient Order of the Retired—each in his favourite chair, each with well-shined spittoon to hand—inspects the arriving teams with disapproval, or—rarely—with approval.

"Hugh MacLean ain't groomed them bays for a week, looks like." The spittoons splash an echo.

"Ain't no wuss than most. Bud Atkins' boy allus has his hame straps loose. Look at that'n."

Old Angus MacEachran from St. Andrews says his bit: "And would you look at they big anes wi' the old wagon? Och, now, the gelding this side iss spotted like a turkey egg—it'll be a colt from the Glencarnock stud . . ."

A whining crunch interrupts my reverie. The square of sky is blotted out, as a great red truck rolls onto the scales. Suddenly there is music; and the tune is still the tune of the Bain wagon and the jangling, winking harness. It is "Buffalo Gal," and it emanates from somewhere in the upper sanctuary of the great juggernaut. Evidently the driver has tuned in on an "old-time" programme.

The teasing refrain sets my feet a-tapping. From above comes a voice—and, like the music, the voice could belong to the old days. "If you want to dance to my music, fellah, it'll cost you!"

I look up into the face of the High Priest of the Great Red Demon—and *it* is the same, too. The humourous eyes, all etched about with tiny lines, speaking of summer heat and winter frost, belying the grim set of the jaw, a legacy from the years of drought and hail and grasshoppers, of hanging on to things when so many were letting go. The whole long, lean, aging six feet of prairie man is living history. It was Mr. G., from north of Marieton, and from his lips hung a cork-tipped cigarette.

A five-inch snowfall came and laid for two cool days; but it turned milder, and within a week the snow was gone, leaving a damp chill in the air. The respite was brief, and soon ice began to make at the lake edge, tinkling in the dawn breeze; and the swans left, streaming south under leaden skies which brought a foot of soft snow to cover all the taller reeds.

Once, the village youngsters would have thought of their snow-shoes, and boys and girls together would have left the patterns of their rackets in and out of the brush and over the hills. But the snowshoes hang dusty and cracked with age in attics and sheds, for—like the moccasins which were worn then—they have been discarded.

I believe there is a revival of snowshoe clubs in some places, and I hope this invigorating, typically Canadian form of exercise will be popular again. It gives the greatest feeling of well-being to stride loose-limbed over the drifts on a sunny winter's day, when the trees gleam with hoarfrost. Snowshoes add to your buoyancy, for under their elastic mesh the snow is no impediment, but rather complements swift and easy movement.

The Indians of the North make good snowshoes, narrow and upturned in front, which seem to guide themselves between the brush clumps and shrubbery. These are the "trail shoes" made of birch and laced with moosehide *babiche*.

The best moccasins are also Indian-made, consisting of golden-brown moosehide, redolent of the smoke which both softened and coloured them. However, the trade moccasins with laces and eyelet holes serve very well. These are made of chrome-tanned cowhide, and are still available. But not many pairs are sold any more, and they may pass away.

It seems only the other day that all children, as well as teenagers, wore them from freeze-up to spring; and very nice they looked, with the heavy outer sock turned down over the top to keep out snow. The youngsters of those days all had a good carriage that was induced by walking and running in footgear that followed the natural shape of the foot.

Silton is typical of hundreds of tiny villages which mushroomed in the age of settlement along the new railway lines that stretched their tentacles all over the West. Some of these hamlets became towns, others have held their own, but many, like Silton, suddenly found themselves shrinking with the march of progress and the movement to urban centres.

It is the motorcar that has altered the whole rural scene. It was for car owners—especially commercial travellers and businessmen —that the straight hardtop roads were built, and the effect of these on village life has been as disastrous as their side effects on the railways. Firstly, the roads made it possible for the travelling

public to call at the small points, do their business, and be on
their way without an overnight stop. Hotels could not be supported
by the limited patronage that was left. Indeed, if it were not for
the beer-parlour licences, no hotels could stay in operation except
in the large towns. Secondly, the cars made it easy for the farmers
to trade in the city in no more time than it formerly took to visit
the village with horses. The village dwellers followed suit, for distant pastures are lush and green. Thirdly, the bus companies
found that because of this they had few passengers from the
smaller points, and therefore they abandoned service to many of
them, since the new highways also bypassed them. This forced
village dwellers who did not have cars to buy them, for at this
same time the railway companies discontinued passenger service
on many local lines.

Thus was centralisation brought about, and if our main road
and power line from Regina were blown up we would be without
bread, without the paper, without the mail, even without light and
heating. In fact we could be starved out in a week.

The final result, then, was that many small establishments
closed. There is no profit in a drugstore when people buy their
aspirins and shaving lotion from Regina; no need for a blacksmith's shop when there are no longer horses to be shod or plow-
shares to "lay"; no need for a barber or a cobbler or a livery-
stable man; and with the great wagons rotting in barnyards, no
need for a wheelwright.

No place for small farmers, either. The new, shiny tillage implements must cover many more acres than are contained within
a quarter section if they must pay for themselves—which they
may not do before they themselves are obsolete, so rapidly do
fashions in these things change. There are acres of "bone yards"
near our cities crowded with the derelict steam tractors of yesterday, hauled there while twenty or thirty years of service still remained in them. Cheek by jowl lie still useful gasoline tractors of
older make and horse rakes and ploughs. Some of these were sold
to Japanese junk dealers and thrown back at our soldiers in
Singapore and Malaya.

And the modern implements are serviced by telephone communication with Regina, waited on by high-priced acolytes.

So the process of centralisation went, till the springs of community life almost dried up, and neighbour met neighbour more commonly on Eleventh Avenue than on the trail or in the village.

The new system is very efficient. The poor are more easily taken care of in the city, and their relief money far exceeds the wages they would get as farm workers.

As for those who remained in the country, they can jump in a car, rain or shine, hot or cold (defying the hazards of the road), run into Regina, pick up repairs, groceries, haircuts, do their banking, see their lawyer, go through the clinic, all in one trip.

Yet efficiency is not always satisfying. When the local butcher closed shop, you no longer had him as a confidant on meat problems or as a personal friend. You couldn't talk about the fattest steer he ever saw or the fine lambs he had bought.

In the city you don't know the clerk who serves you. You don't know his politics, his religion, his background, his interests. You are served, and you leave.

Or you take your car to a city garage. You don't know the mechanic who works on it, nor the owner, nor the man at the desk who gives you the bill. You pay; but if you are not pleased with the result you can't tie anyone down. They say: "Oh, I guess Elmer worked on it—he's gone home now."

There is no *contact,* as there was with the livery-barn man who knew the names of everyone's horses—their age, colour, breeding; who warned you of a blizzard coming, and you listened to him if you were wise.

So the breach between town and country widened, until today the two constitute very nearly "two solitudes." One almost longs to hear the ring of an anvil, to see the patient hip-shot horses awaiting the farrier's attention, to see a livery barn standing in brave red paint with its whinnying teams and smell of sweet hay, instead of today's garage with the broken-down cars sitting helpless in the weed-grown rear.

As Mr. Metcalf, retired pioneer (born in Prince Edward Island), said to me the other day, "They should never have let them build those big tractors. If they had kept them small we could have more people in work.

"Everybody goes to the city, and they study and study from books till they lose the meaning of life."

The natal cord binding the craftsman and the merchant and the cultivator, of which I have spoken, has been broken, and the "gap between knowledge and wisdom" widens.

The separation of urban and rural life into two solitudes began many years ago, with a renaissance become worldly and a reformation turned sour, and the rise of the industrial revolution set the course for the pattern of today. Divorced from the country, from natural law, we began to lose touch with the cause of craftmanship, which through our thoughts and hands transmuted the riches of the earth into riches of the spirit and the aesthetic sense. Milton flared like a candle, but his light was dimmed when revolutionary France set up the worship of Reason on her altars. Already the brief shaft of Hellenic light which had lit the Elizabethan Age had been replaced by the bright neon sign of commerce, and the intellectuals who became its mouthpiece cared little that rural England—the Merry England of the corn harvest and the shepherd—would suffer decay as it followed this new sign.

This Empire of Commerce did not wish to see the continuance of the self-contained rural scene which operated freely and locally. As Burke wrote: "The age of chivalry is gone, that of sophisters, economists and calculators has succeeded [it]."

It was as if the barons had never withstood King John. The barons themselves were now the traders, the importers, the packagers, and their fortresses the roomy but close-knit offices of centralisation.

The feudal system forced men to work, but now the reign of bureaucracy has denied men the right to work. The serfs were required to stay in their villages, but now they are forced to leave, to the uprooting of whole towns.

The country parson of Chaucer's day became the beneficed cleric in his big house at the edge of the denuded village, and, with too much time on his hands, became the fox hunter, yoiking through the coverts. Worldliness had taken the clergy by the throat with the rise of the industrial revolution. They should have protested against the signs which pointed to the scattering of their flock, but by now it was too late. It was too late for the squire, too, who had thought to raise his "standard of living" by investing the proceeds of farm and field in new commercial enterprises, which would doom that farm to enclosure, as the flood of cheap corn from overseas began to compete.

Parson and squire found themselves enclosed indeed, like the sheep. The flocks lacked a shepherd, but the shepherd of souls lacked a flock; and the squire, now committed, had to watch the stock market rather than his men swinging the scythe.

And a once happy religion was separated from daily life and daily tasks. Men do not sing in factories as they watch the bobbins turn, and there is little to remind them of God in the narrow rows of tenements they must occupy. God is no longer around, but packaged, and as hard to get at as a cigarette in its cellophane wrappings—there is only the gin shop round the corner.

Who spoke for the sanctity of the home, for the cotter's Saturday night? For the quiet evenings by the fireside, Mother with cat on lap, knitting perhaps, as she read to the children about the Snow Queen, Alice, or Jo's Boys? Who cares now that Gerda's feet were cold as she took the lutefisk to the Lapland woman? Where are the tears which washed from Kay's eyes the glass splinter of the technocratic mirror? Who even knows that Hans Andersen could see and feel these things? But Mother tucked her brood up for the night, while her man put out the cat and stoked the stove against the coming night.

Woman the Mother; Father the Priest of the Hearth.

The readings, the talks, the simple daily chores. It was these that moulded the character of free men; that taught obedience, initiative, courage, and uprightness.

There is an ancient legend of the Carpathians of a people who had their heads down grubbing for gold. They were conquered by horrible beings, fat and soft, all head and stomach. These kept the people herded, grovelling and grunting on all fours on the grazing grounds, fattening them like so many pigs, breeding them like cattle. The guards, the herders, were jackasses, who prevented the herd from thinking by their constant braying. Any that tried to stray were punished by lashing hooves and chased back to the herd with wicked teeth.

Silton is luckier than some villages.

It still has a primary school which children of the area attend, but last year it closed its high school and lost a good principal, for now grades Nine to Twelve are bussed up highway No. 20 to Strasbourg.

Silton has a triweekly train, but it is for freight only, where once you could go down to Regina in the morning and back at night on a fast passenger. The bus can be used, but it is inconvenient unless you wish to leave your car locked up two miles from the village.

The elevator operates and, by the way, the grain buyer, Mr. Kowalyshyn, has for several years in succession been the recipient of the prize for the best-kept premises in the division.

There is a telephone exchange in a dwelling house, and a post office—also in a private dwelling. The postmistress is Mrs. Cowen, but there are so many of that name in and around Silton that Hope and I, between ourselves, have adopted the Welsh system of differentiation, and speak of her as Cowen-post-office. There is also Cowen-farmer and Cowen-oil-man. The latter operates a fuel-oil business and, as a side line, an implement agency. His two little children—a boy and a girl—love to play on "Daddy's tractor," which sits across the road on a patch of grass.

There is a large general store which does a surprising lot of business, which is increased in summer by visitors from the weekend cottages at nearby Cook's Beach and Cowen's Beach and Saskatchewan Beach and Pelican Point and Glen Harbour to the west.

This store is the principal village meeting place. It is large and roomy, with masses of merchandise on the shelves, on the floor, in the big windows; or hung from the ceiling.

Here you can buy the things country people still use—water pails and cans, clotheslines and clothespins, brooms, ropes and wire. Here one sees no anxious, harried faces; there is no push and hurry, no exclamations of annoyance. People saunter in, pass the time of day, look about them for what they want—all with the air of visiting a neighbour's house.

Not that there is any lack of efficiency.

True, the big roll-top desk in the corner is surrounded by a veritable barricade of catalogues, price lists, and old files in cardboard boxes, apparently thrown up as higgledy-piggledy as a boy's fort or earthwork; but Alex Burrows, the High Priest who presides over this collection, knows exactly where everything is. A modern adding machine rests easily on a few piled-up books, and a typewriter clacks where one would expect to hear the squeak of a goose quill.

There is behind one window a wire to which are clipped notices of Church Suppers, the Game Laws, and those bright-coloured, fascinating lists of goods and cattle for sale which the local auctioneer changes so frequently.

What they do not have on hand at the store they will gladly fetch you from the city, so you need not trouble yourself with writing or purchasing money orders. In addition to this service, the store acts as banker to many.

Some of the summer folk, inured to city ways, have suggested the conversion of this establishment to a "serve yourself" supermarket, but so far this suggestion has not borne fruit. It would mean curtailment of the services mentioned, and much of the flavour would be lost; nor could the farm housewife phone in an order, have it filled, and pick it up at leisure.

The store is in the hands of one family—two brothers and a sister—who, with a sister-in-law, operate the whole concern. It is a successful example of free enterprise. The profits do not go outside the community, and since we have become aware to what extent centralisation has diluted the local scene, we have reached the point of resistance.

Undoubtedly one thing which forced a good many small merchants to the wall in days gone by was the mail-order catalogue. I remember, in the twenties, how Mr. Mattenly, the general merchant at the village of Young, told me that farmers who owed him up to thousands of dollars would, from the sale of their first wheat delivery in the fall, send large cash orders to Eatons at Winnipeg. He should have known; he was also the postmaster, and he sold them the money orders. Ever since this was pointed out to me I, personally, have steadfastly refused to send money out of whatever settlement I reside in. Most of the goods people send for are on the shelves in their home store. Indeed, I know many merchants who have the mail-order catalogues under the counter for comparison.

Last but not least, Silton can boast a village well, slap in view between the big white store and the old railway station.

At this well you will see, on a hot summer's day, the new Dodges, the shining Volvos, and the Ramblers of the cottage folk who line up with pails and cans to take turns at the complaining pump; for there is a dearth of good water at the beaches, and they must carry home our silver-pure product to provide their cool drinks.

Most water sources are brackish with alkali in this land, and children are notoriously thirsty folk, so in spite of the new power line and the bright electric lights, the village pump must fulfill its ancient task.

Silton is satisfied to have her well, and she willingly shares it with the neighbours, in an unbroken tradition. Only yesterday their fathers saw the daughters of Zion fill their water pots from the wells redug by Isaac, as today we see the women of Silton, coifed against summer's heat or winter's cold, trip to our village pump in anticipation of their cup of tea. A well—a hand-dug well —is not a status symbol, not a gadget, not perhaps a technological success; but it holds need and purpose in its cool depth. We may find better ways of providing water, but we shall never find a substitute for it, and while it may be good to be able to name this element according to its chemical formula it is much more satisfactory to know its uses—and use it.

"Dear sister water," said St. Francis—for he perceived the ecological fact of our dependence on its purifying and cleansing properties.

It has been said that all roads lead to Rome, but in our natural environment to follow a path—of man or beast—is to come eventually to the water hole, the pond, the well. Here are the ancient meeting places, here a truce reigns, here people pass the time of day, and here they enjoy *contacts* which are entirely absent from the sink tap of the city.

November is a very revealing month, for the fall of the leaves has unrobed the trees, and now the secrets of summer stand stark —the nests of orioles pendant from the upper branch, the homes of catbirds snug in the shrubbery, the great stick nests of magpies, crows, and hawks in many a bluff, black as a raven's wing against the sky.

The trees and scrub on our village lot are of the native varieties, and obviously the builders removed only what was necessary for them to manipulate the timbers and lumber and allow for a small lawn in front and a drying ground behind. So Hope, hanging up the weekly wash, is able to see no less than two orioles' nests, a cedar waxwing's, and a kingbird's.

It is with less joy that we see, nakedly exposed, the bits of Kleenex brought here by the wind and caught up in the base of the bushes; or with a guilty conscience realise that the empty oil can and the discarded carton we thought were out of sight are in full view of passers-by. How easily do we create our own slum conditions; how thoughtlessly do we, in the calm assurance that Kleenex is the answer to problems of hygiene, throw our germ-laden tissues from the car. With grey skies and cold November winds the scene is sufficiently dreary without the addition of such eyesores!

It is time to bring the storm windows from the cellar and remove and store the fly screens. This is now the main part of the autumn chore of getting ready for winter weather.

It is cold on the ladder, but it is nice to finish the job all shipshape and be called in for a cup of tea. As I went in, a bright-faced boy went by and gave me a happy grin. He was wearing a pair of cowhide moccasins, and pulled a sleigh with two cans of water for his mother.

CHAPTER IX

December—The Moon of Feasts

One reason why Silton is so peaceful and quiet is that there is no longer a hotel, and therefore no beer parlour—or, as they say now, beverage room. Today public drinking is a far worse thing, for too often in the West it is so surrounded with regulations that it becomes a rather gloomy matter of seeing how much beer can be consumed in a given time. Customers must remain seated. There is no easy mixing, because each table has to keep to itself. Bad as they were, the old pre-war bars may have been better. Men came in, stood at the bar, tossed off a drink, and went out. But these were closed in 1915.

There is some home drinking in our village, but this is on a small and abstemious scale, and actually many people do not "indulge," as they say, at all.

The village is, in general, based on Methodism, and, while the church of that name was long ago merged with a section of the Presbyterians and most of the Congregationalists, the Wesleyan Methodist flavour persists; but not in a narrow kill-joy sense, and it is no secret that some of the retired farm couples are not above making a little wine for their stomachs' sake. That made from saskatoons is not unlike port, and is usually served quite ceremoniously as a special treat. Rhubarb, chokecherries, and other fruits are also used, and some of the recipes go back many years, like the words which you still hear in the kitchens. I have heard "receipt" for "recipe," "apern" for "apron," and "pattren" for "pattern" by a queer exchange of "r's." More than one lady I know will still speak of "redding up" the house.

Close to the store is a long, grey building used as a community hall. Just behind is a smaller Legion Hall, witness to the large number of old soldiers of three wars who are still in the neighbourhood.

These, with the churches, indicate a certain traditional way of life which has been stubbornly maintained by the few businessmen and retired farmers who constitute the Village Council. A way of life which consists of attending church together, as well as patronising all the various turkey suppers and sales of work put on by the good ladies of the church groups. If one afternoon you should see a lot of cars parked before the Village Hall, just walk in, and you will find the farmers and their wives drinking tea and eating cakes. At a long trestle table you will observe quite a collection, starting at one end with pickles, preserves, jams, tarts, cakes, and homemade candy, and gradually passing through the stages of knickknacks, tea cosies, and "worked tablecloths" to "oven mitts," aprons, and bathmats. These are for sale, and the ladies behind the table will take your money, wrap up your purchase, and give you a nice country smile for good measure.

If you are a man, and if you are wise, you will seat yourself at a table of farmers, for you can sip your tea, eat your cake, and light a smoke in careless ease, while the conversation flows easily around the topics of weather, crops, and stock.

The ladies at their tables are then left free to discuss much more important matters, which may involve the number of hours spent under an anaesthetic!

There are no less than three churches in the village.

A tiny Roman Catholic chapel is closed all winter, but is served in summer by a priest from Saskatchewan Beach, where there is a cottage used by the Jesuit Fathers of Campion College for weekend rests during the holidays.

There is an equally small Evangelical Lutheran church for the spiritual comfort of the German Canadian settlers from east of town, and this is served by a hard-working and devoted pastor who, for all he looks and talks like a peasant farmer, is a good shepherd for his flock.[1]

But both of these chapels are overshadowed by the much larger United church, which stands on higher ground.

Anglicans must in theory go twelve miles up the "angling road" to the church at Marieton which I have mentioned before, or else down to the valley to the church at Craven. But many in practice prefer not to risk the icy roads and blowing snow of winter, and are happy to worship with the United folk. After all, the differences are mainly based on doctrinal points of view, and we remember that John Wesley was reared and lived an Anglican, and in spite of the dig at him by the otherwise saintly Hawker of Morvenstow (*John Wesley came into Cornwall and persuaded the people to change their vices*), he left a deep sense of personal spirituality with us, even if he lost us much of the riches of the liturgy. Whether we do or do not make the Sign of the Cross, whether we pray kneeling, standing, or sitting, forms are not essential and can matter little in the Courts of Heaven, since the promise that where two or three are gathered in the Name must hold good.

Each of these churches has its Ladies' Auxiliary and young people's group, while in addition there is a Red Cross group, a 4-H Club, and, of course, the Legion with its Auxiliary.

So we attend each other's bazaars and sales, rarely enquiring whether they be for this or that, just as we attend each other's services. In true village life everyone is your neighbour, and no one can isolate himself as you might in a city. The whole is responsible for the part, and the parts for the whole.

The small Village Council, the local School Board—these are the training grounds for service; these are the local foundations upon which good government is built, and we are sad to see how fast they are passing in this age of centralisation.

Let it not be thought that our people lack gaiety or eschew pastimes—far from it. There is a curling rink, and the majority of the people attend there with the same regularity with which they go to church. The ladies are real curling fans; in fact, the elder (Grandma) Cowen tells me she played there to the age of seventy.

One wonders that she stopped then, for at over eighty-five this remarkable woman of many parts still marches to the store with the firm step of her Grenadier grandfather! After she lost her husband she had to take over the family farm, and I am told it was no uncommon thing to see her in the dead of winter striding over the prairie on snowshoes, looking for her horses.

To return to the curling rink. The present long, low lumber building replaces an earlier one famous for having been built for the expenditure of only a few nails. Apparently with money scarce in the years of the Great Depression ("the dirty thirties"), under pressure to arrange for their own recreation, the menfolk of Silton hauled hay bales and poplar poles and built a roomy curling rink without benefit of cement, lumber or roofing material. By courtesy of the Canadian Pacific Railway an old boxcar was obtained and set up at the entrance to make a sort of lounge lobby, complete with stove, so that contestants and onlookers could warm themselves. To avoid danger from flying sparks, the stovepipe was topped with an old gasoline barrel furnished with a wire screen. However, this precaution did not save the building, for after it had been in use some years it did finally burn to the ground. Someone had carelessly set a fire to destroy a patch of weeds, and this got out of control, so that before it could be stopped the hay walls of the rink were ablaze.

But the homemade affair had served its purpose, and by that time the community was able to afford the new lumber building we use today.

Just south of our house, next to the school, are several vacant lots. This area is level and low-lying, and provides a playground for football in summer, but in winter it is used for an outdoor hockey rink. A well close by, and provided with a pump, is the source of the water with which the rink is flooded as soon as freeze-up comes. This water is too alkali to drink and is used only for this purpose. From our front window we can watch the youngsters as they skate in pursuit of the puck, faces glowing as brightly as the toques and scarves they wear. On the sidelines big sisters hold tottering small brothers, or little groups of budding stick wielders play shinny with whatever they can find to knock about. Since the disappearance of horses such things are not so easily come by.

On rough days, after a snow-and-wind storm has piled big drifts across the shimmering green ice, we see the bigger boys and girls frantically and in joyous abandon scooping the snow away into great piles to the side. We hear their laughter as the blood courses through them; we see the rosy cheeks whipped by the winter wind. It is a labour of love they perform—a sort of challenge to be met, which their city cousins know little of. On the really cold below-zero days, the girls may not be there, but still the boys, to show their sturdy young manhood, perform what, but for the spirit of adventure, would be a menial task. This is the very heartbeat of the Canadian scene, one which contributes to our country's existence as much as the playing fields of Eton to the British Isles.

Community dances were very much a part of early pioneer life as I first knew it.[2] As settlers got better established and built larger houses and more of them took wives, it became customary to have more or less regular neighbourhood parties at different houses in turn. Usually a Swede or an Irishman could be found to play the fiddle, or perhaps a German or Russian would bring his accordion; and then, if room permitted, there would be some dancing. Otherwise, perhaps there would be a song from one, a story from another, a recitation, or a step dance. Jack MacLeod was the man for that; bent and gnarled from years in the Michigan lumber camps, Jack, once warmed up, was a wizard with any old shanty tune such as "The Curse of Michigan," which was a favourite song of his.

A plump little Quaker woman used to sing in a little-girl voice "It's a Story from Life's Other Side," in a way to bring tears to your eyes.

Other favourite songs were "The Cowboy's Lament," "Swanee River," and "Silver Bells." Robert Service's poems, especially

"The Cremation of Sam McGee," ranked high as recitations. A hulking young homesteader, formerly a Barnardo boy, used to give us "The Ancient Mariner."

Within a very few years, kiddies were getting old enough for school; and with the building of the brand-new schoolhouse a new phase of community life opened up, for here at last was room for a real dance.

The folks came in anything from a team and bobsleigh with a straw-filled wagon box, in which a family of half a dozen could cover themselves with robes and keep warm, to single-seated cutters for courting couples and saddle horses for bachelors. Great was the competition to get one's horse into the small school barn; and, when one got there early and achieved this, great was the impossibility of getting him out again until several late-comers had first removed their mounts. The animals would be jammed in so tightly that it was impossible for them to kick or otherwise hurt each other.

Someone was usually at the schoolhouse early to keep the fires going. Dances were commonly held on Friday night, as there was no school on Saturday; this meant that there was plenty of time to clean up the schoolroom, as well as for the participants, including the schoolmarm and the pupils—many of whom had to come with their parents, as they couldn't stay home alone—to lie abed the next morning. Women with families brought the youngsters, unless they were lucky enough to have someone to stay home with them; so sleeping babies and small tots were apt to be stacked up pretty thick in the cloakroom, and one had to be careful about stumbling around looking for overshoes or mitts. Nursing mothers had to attend to babies between dances, and the bachelors soon found out that a lady sitting in the corner of the cloakroom with a shawl over her shoulders wasn't sulking, didn't have a headache, and needed no other help than to be left alone.

Every lady brought a box containing sandwiches and cake; and when, as often happened, these affairs were "box socials" in aid of the Red Cross or some other charity, the boxes were auctioned at suppertime. High prices were sometimes paid for a recognized and finely decorated box, because the purchaser had the privilege of partnering the lady at supper. But many were the disappointments too, because the crafty auctioneers were fond of encouraging the bids by broad but misleading hints that such and such a box was the work of such and such a popular young lady. The bachelor who was prepared to spend the most money was often in for a surprise when he found that his partner was not pretty Helen Boychuk, but toothless old Mrs. Soderquist. But it was always taken in good humour, and he knew how to carry off his mistake with a flourish, with flattering compliments to the said Mrs. Soderquist. So stoutly would he claim to have known all the time that it was her box that he would come to believe it himself, and boast that he knew good cooking and good company and would choose it every time before a pretty face and soggy sardine sandwiches!

Coffee was contributed in raw state and boiled up on the schoolhouse stove. And such coffee!—especially if it was prepared by a good Swede woman who knew just how it should be. Of other refreshments, little appeared officially; but various odd-shaped bottles would be tucked under buggy robes, and when their owners got too dry they and their cronies stepped out into the frosty air for a snort.

Sometimes, but rarely, the odd chap would indulge a bit too freely, and perhaps raise a row about something, usually accusing some other man of dancing too much with his girl. This often meant a fight; but that was usually pushed off into the background, well out of sight—somewhat to the disappointment, I fear, of the girl concerned.

Of course, men were in the majority; so the women, regardless of their age, were almost danced off their feet. Music was still the fiddle, but it was often helped out by chording on the piano, if the school boasted one. For that reason most of the dancing was of the real high-flying, old-fashioned style, for your fiddler balks at syncopation. The dance tunes, like the dances themselves, came from many sources. They varied from Russian polkas to Swedish steps picked out to the tune of "Life in the Finland Woods";

from the Irish and Scottish tunes used for square dancing to "The Red River Reel"—a truly Canadian tune of the *voyageurs*—and importations like "Buffalo Gal."

In couple dancing, favourite of course was the old-style waltz. There was always one at half-time called the "supper waltz," and another at the end called the "Home, Sweet Home," and danced to that tune. Every man claimed his proper partner for that; and many and devious were the tricks played by some partnerless young man to have a rival lured behind the barn for a drink, so that he could claim the lady with the unblushing lie that her real partner had pulled out for home.

But besides the waltzes there were many dances never heard of in the cities; and to this day they are cherished and danced to by prairie dwellers. There was the Jersey, to which toughened old men loved to shake a foot and bend and swing in graceful time; the seven-step, which tells you how all good children go to Heaven; the two-step; the three-step; the various thumping, dizzy polkas; the gallant French minuet, danced to "Coming Through the Rye," and the graceful waltz called La Rinca.

But still—except for perhaps the very youngest set—the squares were the supreme achievement. "Couples for a square!" would cry a sweating man in blue serge with his collar open, and the men would straighten from lounging against the wall and go across to the ladies cooling off on the opposite benches, bowing gallantly and "making a leg" before leading their ladies on to the floor to arrange the square. "Four more couples wanted!" the sweating M.C. would shout again. It was he who "called" the dances—and how he could call, in time, to "Turkey in the Straw" or "The Irish Washerwoman"! "Tiddle-um-tee-tum, tiddle-um-tee-tum" went the fiddlers, and as the couples bowed you heard the M.C.'s voice again in a high sing-song. *"First* couple up to the right and dosey-do . . . Pass right through . . . *On* to the next and dosey-do . . . *Ladies* join your lily-white hands and gents your black and tan . . . Ducky dive on the ocean wave . . . Hawkie fly out and give birdie a swing . . . *Meet* your own and pass her by . . . *Kiss* the next one on the sly . . . Promenade to you know where."

They all worked hard, but no one harder than the M.C., who had to keep his ear on the music and his eyes on the perhaps four or five "sets."

And if the dancers flagged there was always Pat to give us "Me Grandfather's Ould Leather Britches," or some ex-lumberjack to step to the high, stirring notes of "The Devil's Hornpipe," before we all went back again to "Turkey in the Straw."

Winter nights are long on the prairies, and with the everlasting winds the trails drift over in a few hours. Few merrymakers care to head for home in the dark and risk overturning in a snowbank or losing the trail—as I have known happen—and wandering about for hours; so all hands usually kept up the good work till daylight.

Finally someone would shout: "Daylight coming!" and looking out we would see the rime-crusted heads of horses sticking out patiently from their blankets as the reflected beams of the not-yet-risen sun touched the tips of the snowdrifts. "Home, Sweet Home" would be called, and cut short as couples left the floor; and there would be a scurry for quilts and robes, a wakening of sleepy-eyed children to wrap them up like so many mummies, while the menfolk hitched up the horses amid musical jingle of harness bells.

And so homeward, with many a "Had a grand time" or "Didn't Jack step lively to the fiddle tonight?"—or, from some sleepy bundle, "Momma, are we going home now?"

And so away over the blown-in trails, with a frosty creak of sleigh runners, each vehicle branching off to its own small home across the snowy plain.

Soon would come seeding time and no more dancing, because the toil on the land would take every minute not spent in sleeping; but many a young chap, as he whistled "Turkey in the Straw" to the creak of his seed drill, would look forward to another winter—another season of jollification in the little schoolhouse.

But today, the car has spoiled that too; and we no longer hold dances at Silton. In a community as close to the city as we are they have died out for the simple reason that they ceased to be community affairs. Word of a dance would get out—as it always does—and up from Regina would roar the cars full of young people who thought that in the country, among the hicks, they could behave as they liked. It was the mentality of soldiers on foreign service, of the townee let loose in the country with a game licence; rejoicing in freedom far from the critical eyes of relations and friends.

So these young folk thought they could take over the show. They demanded jazz and boogie-woogie and rock-'n'-roll. They shouted, they screamed, they gave orders to the orchestra. Meanwhile the older people shifted uncomfortably on the sidelines. It was *their* dance, too, for we do not run in age groups in the country.

Aunts and uncles, even grandmothers, were waiting for that square dance or that waltz to which they had looked forward all week.

The cars from the city carried booze as well as youngsters. Not the modest bottles of home brew which used to be sipped by men only in the privacy of the horse barn, but cheap gin from the liquor store.[3] And it was the young folk from outside—boys and girls both—who helped themselves from the flasks between dances. Couples slipped out to the waiting cars and snuggled up, and then returned—and eyebrows were raised, for that was against the code of the country, which insists that no girl should ever leave the hall except in company with another girl or woman.

The mothers feared for the sunburnt sons who were coming under the spell of the glamorous strangers—girls with their cheap perfume and cheaper jewelry. The young farmers, unskilled in the latest dance steps, glowered from the sidelines as they saw their sisters and their sweethearts blushing under the advances of the city slickers—who were quite likely living on unemployment insurance, because that is easier than working.

And the next thing you knew, there was a fight, for the country boy did not care to see his sister plied with drink—or dance with a drunk—and the evening was spoilt, and the party broke up—if, indeed, it was not broken up by the police.

On the streets of Regina I heard one punk tell another that there was a dance at a village some miles away.

"Yeah?" The other droop nodded. "Let's go and raise Cain!"

Silton put a stop to raising Cain—but we miss the old-time fun.

Shortly before Christmas our fuel-oil man called on us to fill our basement tank. There is great comfort in an oil furnace, electrically controlled and manipulated by a simple thermostat in the living room—at least, till the power fails. Then we must revert to the traditional type of heating. I have been able to obtain a wood stove, which will be set up as an auxiliary. Also a coal-oil lamp and a lantern. We were left in the dark not long ago, and I had to go over to the store for candles. The storekeeper, too, was peering about with a flashlight, looking for *his* coal-oil lamp.

Our fuel-oil man simply backs up his truck, uncoils his hose, and in a few minutes two hundred gallons of oil are in our basement. This is certainly easier than packing in wood, yet I rather miss that chore. Wood is clean and sweet and full of memories. When you fill the woodbox it is almost as if you had brought in the world of nature. Here are the green sticks full of sap; there the dry, lichened and knotty. Sometimes you even get a piece of poplar with a woodpecker's hole bored in it.

Up to a few years ago, this was the season for the farmers whose woodpiles were low to go to the bluffs with sleighs and teams and cut dry wood for immediate use. Later, they would cut the green for another year, and in the spring they would have "sawing bees" and help one another to buzz the long green poles into firewood lengths. They like to split the blocks in frosty weather, for then a sharp tap of the axe is enough to do the job.

When the temperature is above freezing the blocks are dull and sluggish, and the axes become wedged in them.

Then comes the piling, or stacking, and this must be done artistically if grandfather does it. He does the best job, for he retains more of the countryman's patience and pride. Perhaps he comes from Old Ontario, where skillful piling of wood is part of the pattern of good farming. Snow is deep there, but it often is in Saskatchewan, too, and no one wants to grub down in the snow for an armful. Grandfather enjoys the work; he feels he is still useful, still part of the family, and his supper goes down the better for having been earned. He does not hurry; he can pause to puff his pipe and thank God he is not learning to knit in the Old Folks' Home. If he has an understanding family he will do this till he dies. This, too, is a labour of love.

One day we drove east and north to the village of Leross near the Touchwood Hills and saw many of these wood stacks. The best ones are round in shape with straight sides and a conical top. The land about Leross is quite heavy poplar and willow bush, and the farms are smaller—backward, people would say. For this reason much wood is still burnt. We also saw great piles of poplar rails which were being sawed in six-foot lengths, then sharpened and stacked in neat piles ready for the bluestone tanks. These will become fenceposts.

We see little of this now around Silton. We are more "progressive," with our power lines and oil heating. But oil too will pass; for already it is being replaced by natural gas, just as a few years ago oil replaced coal and wood. It is a wasteful process, for you have to tear out and discard expensive equipment each time a change is made. But they tell me that waste is now an absolute necessity if we are to keep up production and at the same time our standard of living.

The trips to the "bush" used to be most enjoyable. You started out after the morning chores, after the sun was up, and broke trail through the snowdrifts. You sat on the empty running gear of your bobsleigh, balancing yourself on the front bunk, which would swing sharply if one end caught against a twig. Your feet were against the steel "knees" where they were bolted to the runners, and if you didn't watch out, a bush or a stump would knock a foot off and you might take a tumble.

Your axe, your bunk stakes, and your logging chain were secured by your stake ropes to the hind bunk.

The wind might be rough and cold, but in the shelter of the bluff you hardly felt it. Strange, that a few acres of leafless poplars can offer such protection.

When you arrived at the trees of your choice, you took off your sheepskin coat and went to work, putting up your bunk stakes on the further side of the bobsleigh only while you loaded your first—and largest—poles. And when you had two or three layers for a "floor," when the poles began to roll off the near side, you put in those two bunk stakes, and thereafter you had to lift your poles over the tops of them.

A little better than halfway up your stakes you tied them together with the ropes to prevent the weight of the load breaking them off as you swung around corners. Then, over the ropes, the balance of the load, fitted to a nicety—three to four feet on the stakes according to the trail; less, perhaps, for your first trip, but after a few loads you would have two twin tracks beaten hard and as slippery as glass, along which your load would glide with hardly a tug from the horses.

But before you started for home you threw your heavy chain around the whole and tightened with a gin pole till the frosty poles squealed and formed a solid mass which could not come apart. You then tied down the end of the gin pole with one of your halter shanks. A properly adjusted and chained load would never slip, and was good for many miles of road.

But it wasn't done that quickly, for at half-time—if you were any distance from home—you stopped to make a little, neat fire, to boil your billycan for tea and to thaw out the sandwiches you had brought.

The team, meanwhile, munched the oat bundles you had also brought (put in a sack they had been a nice cushion against the hard, cold bunk). The horses' heads would be half-lost in the fog from their breath, and every once in a while there would be a jingle of harness bells as one threw up his head to get the collar back against his shoulders.

And as you munched you would look around you and see, perhaps, a downy woodpecker overhead, tapping industriously at a dead branch. Or you would hear a sweet, rising note, and be able to pick out a rosy pine grosbeak all fluffed up and whistling to his smoke-grey wife and family as they foraged among the rose hips at the bluff's edge. Or the team might lift their heads together and blow, and you would follow their gaze and see a young buck show himself at the edge of some scrub. And it was as well, too, to be on the lookout for an irresponsible town-bred hunter, for such as they never expect to see a farmer about his lawful business in what such a hunter thinks of as "the wilds," and he may shoot you or your horses on sight.

There is a tale told to the north of the settlements which concerns such an episode. It seems that a local butcher advertised the fact that he would skin and cut up big game for tourist hunters. One day a man arrived with an animal in his trailer. He asked the butcher if he would dress a moose he had shot. The butcher went out and looked over the animal. He didn't speak. Finally the hunter said: "Well?" The butcher said he'd rather not tackle the job. "Why?" asked the Nimrod. "Can't you skin a moose?"

"I just reckon I can," replied the butcher, "and I could skin that'n for you—only, it's a horse!"

You got home with your load to see the yellow glow of a lamp in the kitchen window. You unhitched the team and put them in. The frost rime glowed on their coats by the lantern light as they tramped into their stalls, and they rubbed the icicles off their lips against the partition posts, making the bells jangle again. You stuffed the manger with sweet hay, and went to supper. The chores could wait till you'd eaten. You had done something few young men could do today. You had practised an art which required an eye for the trail, a judgment for the most desirable trees, a knack to fell them the right way, and the hands, too, for wielding the axe without effort, and the skill to fit the crooked poles with the straight, to balance the load and to guide the plunging team.

Supper sat well.

The winter solstice brings us to the great day of the year, Christmas.

For some weeks the preparations have been going forward, but the old sense of mystery is being lost. "Sandy Claus," as the children call the unseen spirit of loving and giving which surrounds us at this season, now appears not as a midnight visitor, unseen and mysterious, but in human form. Children are actually led to believe that he rewards, in person, their little efforts to be good.

We never had that idea. We knew Father Christmas to be a spirit only. We knew that it was our parents who bought and paid for the Noah's Arks, the books, the balls, and the tops. Santa's job was only to whisper in their ears, and ours too.

And we were not given presents as *rewards*. They were presents —Christmas presents; and there was no question of being good or bad, clever or stupid at schoolbooks. Love does not tie strings to presents.

So we had no need to pass through an unhappy stage of disillusionment, like Stephen Leacock's story of poor Hoodoo McFiggin, which commences by saying that the Santa Claus business is a sneaking underhand method. Santa Claus is as valid to me today as he was in my childhood.

The good gentleman has been put to work like any other advertising medium, to hold court in city stores at so much a day. The youngsters ask for things beyond their parents' resources, and the end result is either a child with a grudge against Santa or a parent feeling inadequate.

And when the youngsters do discover the hoax—but, there, it's Stephen Leacock's story.

We should have left the mystery alone. But this cannot be, so long as Mammon rules—to disenchant us in the end.

A little city girl, sharing our young daughter's new picture book, called her mamma. "Oh, look, Mother!" The lady looked long and hard at a lovely coloured picture of gauzy-winged fairies and said: "Yes, dear, what a lot of pretty little girls!"

For such, who know not the fairies, there can be no Santa Claus; only a paid buffoon in a cotton-wool beard.

By Christmas Day the children have already been to several "Christmas Trees," so the little green spire in the sitting room doesn't look so bright after all. And the children hardly know what a treat is. Once, in hospital at the Joyful Season for the birth of our daughter, Hope heard a visiting lady saying to another lady-in-waiting: "This Christmas shopping is killing me! I've racked my brains, but really the children have *everything!*" Poor little rich children with nothing to look forward to!

The promise of the Child who came to give us life more abundant is in danger of being invalidated by the cynical world which has given us the atomic bomb, so that we must engage in a *danse macabre* before we die.

We are more concerned with remembering the day than the central figure of an event in history. The Name, however, still lives while so much else is forgotten; as the words "Pontius Pilate" hardly commemorate a man, but only a weak act of expediency.

We should be merry indeed. We should laugh, we should feast. We do well to thrill again to the words: "Marley was dead—as dead as a doornail." We do well to remember Tiny Tim. We do well to sing the carols of long ago. But we would do better to silence the voice of commerce in between. And we should first pay our homage to the Giver of all good gifts, and remember that our best gifts to each other are not purchased on the market stalls.

Otherwise we might do better to institute the "Feast of the Merchants" and be done with it, removing it to some other date.

The French Canadians do better than us in this, as in many other respects. They have their secular feast at New Year's. Christmas is for sacred things.

Nevertheless, there will still be many who will remember that Christmas is a Holy Day, many who will worship at Midnight Mass or at Christmas Eve carol services.

The ox and the patient ass have no knowledge, but they once breathed on Wisdom, and they are better company than the jukebox and the bottle.

The shepherd is a lowly, status-less man, but it was those of his craft, unlettered and simple, who in the cold watches of the night were privileged beyond Kings and Emperors.

The crib by the altar touches the soul of every countryman. It is so familiar, so dear to his heart. The rough shed, half dugout; the crude manger, the rustling hay, the warm-blooded beasts, the fowls perhaps roosting on the beams, taking their heads from under their wings and winking in the lantern light, protesting with indignant clucks this intrusion on their time of rest.

Yes, the farmer knows the midnight watches, for his lantern has often revealed the mystery of birth, and the pain and joy of a mother.

Walking home in the crisp December night, with the winking stars casting our shadows softly beside us, we know the meaning of Merry Christmas.

CHAPTER X

January—The Moon of Hunger

This is the month of short days and long nights. It is also the month of most bitter cold.

Yet—in spite of its Indian name—January is not all misery and famine, not even for the Indians themselves, who indeed find hunting not always easy. But they know (in the North) how to camp at a lake where fish are easily caught, as well as how to set their thin rabbit snares among the sheltering willows hard by.

In the South, confined to small reserves, the red people now find little game, but the hand of the Soniow Okimow (the Indian Affairs Department man) is still filled with enough of the "Queen's Bounty" (to quote the treaty talks) to keep actual starvation at bay.

For the wild creatures the worst of the wicked blizzards will still lie ahead in February and March, and, except for the few high winds which drive the snow like powder, they can usually keep comfortable enough beneath their thick coverings of fur and feather.

Consider the snowy owls. Their summer home is in the Arctic, and not only on the mainland coasts, but across that great archipelago of islands ranging northward within wing distance of the Pole. There one may be seen like an "owl in the desert" (for these lands truly are a desert—a frozen desert), sitting atop a hummock or an upthrust outcrop of grey and lichened rock, scanning the soggy northern plain for movements of lemmings or snow buntings or Arctic hare. The wind may howl, the northern mists may carry a chill enough to daunt many a creature, yet this owl keeps his watch and heeds them not. The hot sun alone he avoids and will take shelter from. Only when finally overtaken by the months-long Arctic night does he seek the South. He moves southward not because the prairies are so much less cold, but rather because much of his game has also flitted south or gone into hiding. Thus, on a January morning, we may see one at Silton, perched on a straw stack or a fencepost, against a sky of sullen grey, where he appears all dazzling white.

At our approach he turns his head towards us in unblinking and solemn gaze. We can almost see those wonderful eyes, so round and bright, their orange and black the only touch of real colour— but at this moment he opens his wings and beats away in unhurried flight, swooping low to the ground, then rising easily and calmly to claim another perch. He loves the open country, so like his summer home. He rarely deigns to settle on a tree, for these are not familiar to him, and he still prefers a more solid if less lofty perch, more akin to his lookouts on the barren ridges of his birthplace. And that is why he (being no brush hunter like the goshawk) is found even more often on the open wheat plains towards Regina than he is at Silton.

In winter we rarely see two snowy owls together, for they are solitary birds, each one requiring (or preferring) a good-sized hunting territory to itself. They therefore scatter far and wide across the wide prairies and southward into the Dakotas and Montana.

Some birds are almost immaculately white, but the majority are somewhat flecked with dull black, and quite a few are broadly and plainly cross-barred. Their strong hooked bills, largely concealed by the gape feathers (like bristles), and the huge furry feet concealing ebony talons as long and curved as an eagle's, make them an enemy to be feared by mice and snow buntings and even much larger birds and animals.

I have known one to take a fox.

Since the coyotes have been so poisoned off all over Saskatchewan, the little red foxes have reoccupied much old territory. Recently, when I put up a snowy owl from the top of a rock pile,

I found the still unfrozen and bloody remnants of a vixen on which the bird had been feeding.

Poultry too they may take if they get the chance. But this is not often, for in winter the farmer's flocks are kept pretty well confined.

Where snowshoe hares ("bush rabbits") are plentiful, these rodents probably form the greater part of the snowy owl's diet, but the number of rabbits fluctuates, and in many winters cannot be depended upon, and then the bird must seek the little mice which are the staff of life to so many wild things.

Before following him on this quest, let us look more closely at this beautiful bird. With those big feet, broad wings, and large, smoothly rounded head (for this owl has no "horns" or head tufts), he looks a great deal larger than he really is, as anyone knows who has plucked or skinned one. What we see is 50 per cent feathers (by bulk, not weight), all of which have fluffy bases of purest down, so that he is encased in the original "Arctic Robe" which inspired Mr. Wood, the maker of a first-class sleeping bag.

Even in early spring, with the ice rotting on the lake and the snow half melted, you may still see one of these owls on occasion. He is apt to be by the margin of a lake, looking like a wind-blown newspaper as he squats among the brown reeds. Whether his preference at this time for such a site is for the purpose of keeping cool (for there are still ice floes on the lake), or whether he is watching out for a muskrat or frog or a cast-up fish, I do not know. Perhaps it is a little of both. I have certainly found both fish and frog bones in the pellets he regurgitates when, after the manner of his kind, he rids himself of the accumulation of indigestible fur, feathers, and small bones.

While the deep blanket of snow covering the plains gives an appearance of lifelessness, we would be making a mistake to think that the only living things about are the few snowshoe rabbits in the willows or the jack rabbits whose tracks we occasionally see, or even the rarer coyote who pads by night, hunting.

For under the snow, right down among the grass roots, are the

meadow mice. Not in ones or twos but in hundreds, and indeed—
in some years—in millions. It will not be until spring, when the
snow thaws, that we shall see the nipped-off herbage, the thousands of tiny runways and tunnels, and the little round nests of
grass.

The small rodents are very fond of lawns and leave them
looking quite ragged and patchy, while about the bluffs their work
is equally in evidence; there the grass, the dead leaves, and the
moss are left riddled and worn as a ragged carpet.

In the meantime, while the snow still covers their activities, they
sometimes pop up on warmer days to enjoy the brief noon sunshine, and it is after these sorties that we may see the pattern of
tiny tracks that they have worn on the drifts.

They pose a considerable threat to farmers, especially since
today their natural enemies are much scarcer. In times of abundance (for they are given to population explosions) they overflow
in great numbers from the fields and crowd into sheaf stacks and
store piles of baled hay. Here, besides eating and shelling out and
fouling a good deal of grain, they delight in cutting the binder
string to make their nests. They are also eager for salt, and will
chew to threads anything which contains it, such as bacon rind,
harness, belting—or even old boots and shoes which have been
impregnated with sweat.

Their enemies by day—before deep snow—are hawks, especially
the large buzzards like Swainson's hawk. In spring, mallards
and other ducks will rob nests of micelings. By night, when the
mice themselves are more on the move, they must beware of owls
of all kinds—horned, snowy, long-eared, and especially the low-
flying, ground-hunting short-eared owls.

The few northern shrikes which visit us in winter are also
inveterate mousers. But since they are unable to dig beneath the
snow, they must follow man as he shifts his baled hay or opens
his oat stacks, or else keep company with the coyotes and foxes,
fluttering above them to pounce on the mice as the animals dig
down and disturb them.

By summer the skunks dig out mice nests for the young, but in winter, and by night, it is the foxes, the coyotes, and (in the North) the timber wolves which prey chiefly on them.

All these birds and beasts have been terribly reduced in number by man, who always thinks he can manage nature better than she can manage herself. So we do not have one mousing coyote where once we had, I suppose, fifty. And now, after so many years of facing death by traps, snares, guns, poison, and the gas bait called 1080, after having shown us that they can still maintain a toehold by virtue of their grit and cunning, the coyotes must be harassed by an enemy more deadly than the lot.

It is the snowmobile, a gasoline-motored type of toboggan, capable of great speed over any kind of snow or ice. These instruments of death are commonly known as "skidoos." One day, out walking, we heard the screeching *put-put-put* of some mechanical contrivance. We looked, and soon we saw it—a snowmobile! It was heading across country a mile away, and soon disappeared in a cloud of snow. I asked George at the garage what on earth this black-and-yellow thing was doing out in the fields.

"Oh," said George, "that's whatsisname—he got that thing to hunt coyotes with." He went on to say that whatsisname had already killed a lot of coyotes, and added: "They are sure death. Once you take after a coyote he's had it. You can overtake one in less than a mile, and you don't have to stop to shoot or club. You just run 'em down, right over the top of 'em. If you don't kill 'em first try, you will the second."

This makes the skidoo twice as deadly and effective as the old-time rather sporting way of hunting them with hounds, which were usually a cross of greyhounds with hairy stag hounds. In this hunting the leading hound, on catching up to the coyote, grabs hold of one leg and throws the animal down, whereupon the "killer" hound (usually the largest) leaps at the half-stunned coyote's throat and completes the job. The trouble with hounds is that they hunt by eye, and won't keep a scent or even a track for long. But the man on the skidoo can follow the track if he loses sight of his quarry.

In the old days, the hound hunter followed the chase with his team and single-bob hound box, in which he hoarded his hound's energies until the coyote was sighted. Fences got in the hunter's way, and he would lose valuable time putting down the wire or (to his neighbour's ire) cutting it with pliers. Sometimes, too, the horses got held up in a deep drift and, plunging, broke either the harness or the sleigh pole. Any delay which brought the hunter late for the kill might end in a valueless pelt, for left to themselves the hounds would tear the coyote beyond salvaging.

The snowmobile solves all these problems. Firstly it can travel faster than hounds, and need not give up when the coyote is out of sight. Secondly it does not exhaust itself and can work long hours without a rest. Lastly, being a low vehicle, it can be put out of gear and manhandled *under* a fence in the minimum of time.

We have recently heard of a man who has killed up to four coyotes a day and who at Christmas, by hunting far and wide, already had over twenty coyotes, as well as a fox or two and a bobcat, all of which will mouse no more.

They tell me that usually a coyote will make a burst of speed for a bluff, from which he must be flushed, but after this has been done a couple of times he will not leave the shelter of the scrub, and may be approached and shot there with a .22 rifle.

This is cheap hunting in terms of ammunition, especially in open country, where the snowmobile does the killing job, but it is to be hoped it will prove expensive in terms of breakdowns (and perhaps a long walk home), not to mention the initial cost, for the dealers are blaring the price of this model on the radio daily— about thirteen hundred dollars. It is doubtful whether the coyote supply will last long enough to pay for one, with coyote pelts only eight to ten dollars each. But then, some people are out for "sport," and won't bother to skin them anyway.

Foxes, they say, are harder to get. They "jink" more, are less inclined to run straight ahead, and can make for their earths, where they cannot easily be dug out of the frozen ground. On the wide-open plains many are killed, nonetheless; for three or four snowmobiles working together can surround Reynard.

No wonder the mice increase!

No wonder we no longer hear the happy yaps and barks we heard west of the village last October!

Snowmobiles are being used in the North, too, for hunting caribou and moose and deer on the open muskegs. They can avoid the timber by following rivers, creeks, and lakes. I have reckoned that half-a-dozen snowmobile hunters could kill off what are left of our muskox in one winter! Not to mention their effect on caribou and on that peer of mousers, the timber wolf.

All in all, the snowmobile is a monstrous and horrible invention in terms of wildlife, and one which makes a mock of our coast-to-coast talk about conservation. It should have been left as an army vehicle.

Even the Eskimos are beginning to use this latest invention of the white man to sully the peace of the northland and destroy the last vestiges of antique culture.

Progress?

It is time we tried to keep something of these ancient heritages. It may not be long before you will see a dog team and a stout hickory toboggan only as a show piece!

And, speaking of old things, I have been lately given some priceless treasures of the art of publishing.

They are several half-yearly bound copies of *Cornhill's Magazine,* starting with volumes one and two (1860) and up to 1865. The donor was "Grannie" Cowen, whose husband brought these books from England before the turn of the century. She arrived with them one snowy day, saying: "Here! You're always reading. Keep these old books. My eyes aren't good, and my grandchildren don't want them."

These books were a very welcome gift in January, which is at my age a shut-in month, and, having plenty of time, I have been going through them with joy. There are many delightful contemporary accounts of the great happenings and the explorations of those days, which are as fresh to read as if they had occurred only yesterday.

These books include history, geography, biography, natural history, anthropology, art and music as well as poetry and stories. There is no price on them, but a companion volume, *Sunday at Home,* is even larger and (like *Cornhill's*) completely without advertising matter and with six or seven coloured plates (!) and priced at only one shilling and sixpence a year—not much more than two bits! A perusal of this helps us to see why even the poorest people of England had such a wide general knowledge, even though they might have been short on academic background.

I remember when I was a boy most of the cottage folk and labouring families read this magazine, and as one reads the stories and articles one can see that the supposedly drab and dull Victorian Sabbath was quite the opposite. It would be a strange boy who would rather play cricket on Sunday (something he could do all week) than become absorbed in such fascinating reading.

Many of the contributors one must guess at, for the custom of that day was for writers to be anonymous, but surely (now I am back to *Cornhill's*) I recognise Thackeray and Dickens, Elizabeth Barrett Browning (poetry), Charlotte Brontë, and others.

The "Roundabout Papers" I am sure I recognise, and then there is an unnamed officer of the ship *Fox,* whose "private diary" is really exciting. His "Search for Sir John Franklin" tells how, in 1854, the British Government (being very much engaged with the Russian question) determined that nothing more could be done for the men of the Franklin party, which had been missing since 1846. But in the meantime Dr. Rae of the Hudson's Bay Company brought home intelligence, obtained from the Esquimaux (*sic*) of Boothill Peninsula, of forty white people having been seen on the west coast of King William's Land in the spring of 1850, and that they were travelling southward. At the request of the Admiralty the Hudson's Bay Company in 1855 carried out further investigations, with little success, but even what brief information they were able to gather inspired Lady Franklin to send out another expedition (the fourth).

But it was not until 1857 that the ship *Fox* (steam and sail) was ready and fitted. She left Aberdeen on July 1 that year and sailed first to Friederikshaab in Greenland, then followed coast-wise to Gothaab, where the captain arranged for coal and purchased Eskimo dogs and "sledges."

They cut across Baffin Bay to enter Lancaster Strait and came among the islands. For over two years they explored the area from Pond Inlet to King William's Land, and discovered McClintock Channel (which they named for McClintock, captain of the *Fox*). They divided into several parties for the purpose of exploring in different directions, which permitted the ship's offi-cers at the same time to chart the coastlines of many islands. In this way they covered Somerset, Bathurst, and Prince of Wales islands; but it was in King William's Land (also an island) where they found cairns and skeletons, and a diary giving the date of Franklin's death. The Eskimos assured them that Franklin's party had all perished in their noble and ill-fated attempt to find the Northwest Passage.

An interesting note is struck by the writer's observation that abandoned utensils and guns, as well as clothing, had lain all those years without being touched by the natives. (They may have heard of smallpox!)

It is also interesting to remember that only recently more relics have been discovered to add to our knowledge of the fate of these men, and that a small R.C.M.P. boat, the *St. Roche,* found, and successfully followed, the Northwest Passage from the Atlantic to Wrangel Island off the Siberian coast.

As we read these old accounts and look across the featureless and snow-covered plains of Saskatchewan, we Canadians can realise—perhaps better than other folk—what it must have meant to be isolated for so many years in the Arctic, especially in the days before radio.

As for Captain McClintock and his men—only those of us who

have known the wilderness before the days of wireless, of airplane supply flights, of all the inventions and comforts of modern days (including snowmobiles!), can properly assess the length and breadth of what they accomplished before they dropped anchor more than two years later at the Isle of Wight.

The writer of the narrative I have quoted from mentions one thing which will seem familiar to every old-timer on the plains. He writes: "The wanderings of the Esquimaux can be traced by the circles of stones by which they kept down their skin summer tents." I have heard a modern anthropologist say that the "Indian rings," which I wrote about before, were probably connected with some religious rite or ceremony!

How we do love to labour the obvious and seek to find out more and more about less and less.

When we tire of reading about snow and ice we can turn January to June in our easy chair, simply by picking up any of these volumes. There are accounts of the temples of Rajputana and stories of Lucknow in the days of the Indian Mutiny, with its heat, its blood, and its bravery. Two Canadians won renown at Lucknow. One was the commander of the besieged British forces, Major General Sir John E. Inglis, who was born at Halifax in 1814, son of the Bishop of Halifax and grandson of the first Bishop of Nova Scotia. The other was Private William Hall, a Negro native of Nova Scotia; it was he who found a breach in the wall which allowed the relieving force under Sir Colin Campbell to enter. He earned the Victoria Cross by this act.

Or we can follow Moffat on his missionary activities in unknown Africa, or travel with Livingstone across the Kalahari, over the Ovambo salt plains, where a wheel track can be followed many years after it was made (as later explorers found), to the palm-fringed shores of Portuguese Angola. We can wander south to the plains of Namaqualand and again eastward across Great Bushmanland and the country of the Mashonas, to the great smoky kraals of Chaka and his ebony impis.

All these vivid accounts are by men who were there, not by people who wrote from a week's visit and a month's research.

One thing strikes one in the African accounts, and that is the mutual respect between the whites on the one hand and the tribes on the other. All these writers speak well of the honesty and kindness of these primitive people.

Or again we find these books replete with Canadiana. There are many fine accounts written mostly by British officers and their wives who came to Canada in the line of military or naval duty, many of whom stayed to marry and settle down and leave their blood and their names from coast to coast. They have left us vivid descriptions of old Quebec, of Halifax, and of the Montreal of the first half of the last century. One account of the parties held by the French-English "society" set of old Montreal gives us a pretty glimpse of mid-Victorian Canada.

As for the West, the young R. M. Ballantyne was once a servant of the Hudson's Bay Company, and his descriptions of Fort Garry and the plains of Manitoba, published first in *Cornhill's Magazine,* formed the basis of his *Young Fur Traders,* which inspired so many youngsters of my generation (including myself!) to see the land of Crees and Carioles, of paddles and pemmican.

Had our earlier immigrants been as easily air-borne as the flock of snow buntings now swirling past my windows; had they been free to come and go, to see and return, one wonders how many people would be on these unsheltered plains today?

But there was no return for such as these. They had cut the ties holding them to the Kentish hop fields, the pastures of Shropshire, the mills of Lancashire, and the heather-sweet uplands north of the Tweed. They had to stay, and, staying, learned to love, and, loving, built a future and a family, so that today their seed has become among the envied of the world.

Yet one thinks, if they had gone back, they might not have stayed away. The snow birds will not stay on the southern prairies for long, after the sun strengthens and the creeks run again. For they remember the Arctic, which has lain in darkness so many weary weeks.

They remember King William's Land. They remember the Esquimaux rings. They remember the soft grass of their nest, half buried perhaps in a spot where one might find a blackened, corroded naval button with an anchor upon it. They remember Lancaster Strait and Pond Inlet and the long green grass of the old camping grounds. They remember the howls of the dogs, and cotton grass, and tiny Arctic fireweed, and the yielding moss, and the tramping, clicking feet of caribou.

They remember a harsh land; the sound of ice floes grinding together, the cold ocean mists and the warmth of rocks under the never-setting sun, the mosquitoes. And they remember the dark swift shadow of the snowy owl, and one less bunting to count with the brood.

And they go back. They have to. Nothing stops them.

Today their white beauty greets us, but tomorrow we scan the naked prairie and see them not.

It is the same with us, the prairie folk. We leave and say to ourselves: "We shall see rich grassy meadows and spotted cows, cottage gardens aflame with blossom, sheep-dotted hillsides so green, so green . . ." And we do love them all.

But something calls us.

We have not sweated in these fields. We have not borne the heat of the day in these harvests. We did not build this house with our own hands.

And so we come back to where our own sweat has dimpled the dust fields of midsummer. Where our own feet have trod the furrow. Where we begot our own, and buried our own.

Yes, those who leave must come back. Back to curse the cold. To shake a fist at the wind which blows unhindered from Keewadin to the north, from Hudson's Bay, from the far reaches of the Mackenzie.

Bringing again the snowy owls in silent flight, the buntings in twittering, undulating waves.

Back the women came to take the stiff, frozen clothes from off the line; the union suits looking like naked men swinging from gibbets; the bright towels, striped with red as vivid as the blood of hares spilt on the snowy drifts by an owl's attack.

Back to the warm glow of a simple room, the blinds shutting out the cold and empty night. Back to the books. The stories of our people. The story of our country.

Back to where "He giveth snow like wool and scattereth the hoarfrost like ashes."

In the meantime, we and the wild things are content to wait, for truly the Hungry Month has much with which to fill us, and its passage is swifter than you might think.

CHAPTER XI

February—The Moon of Deep Snows

February fill-dyke, they say in England, and indeed it can be a wet month, as well I remember, when the sou'wester blows up-channel.

But here in Saskatchewan it is usually a month for snow, and as the cloud *weetigos* pluck their geese the white quilt deepens, piling itself on sheds and bins and stacks. Every fencepost is topped with a soft pompom; every twig in the thickets becomes thick and woolly until, as the skies clear and the wind takes possession again, this is caught up and flung whirling like a flock of birds. Very beautiful are these burdened branches, blue against the yellow glow of morning sun; very beautiful are they, too, glowing pink in the evening light. Long are the shadows they cast upon the whale-backed drifts and on the sidewalks by night, etched across the pools of light from the streetlamps.

There are many colours in the snow we so casually refer to as white. These are reflected not intrinsic hues, and they vary according to the weather, the time of day, and the surroundings. With the light in the right quarter, the red side of a shed will warm the snow to pink. If you look against the sun it appears dazzling, yet not quite white, pearly rather, for the snow is not really smooth at its surface, but finely granulated, and since the sun at this season does not climb high enough to look over the top of these tiny hillocks, each one must cast a pinpoint of shadow.

Now turn at right angles to the sun and take a few steps forward. When you look back you find, quite naturally, that the edges of your footprints closest to the sun are in deep blue shadow, but the farther edge, due to its more acute angle to the sun, is so gleaming white that the level untracked snow now looks sullied to that faint griseous hue which is halfway between the intense shadow and the highlight of the footprints.

Next, turn your back on the sun. The tiny points of shadow are hidden, and you are seeing the sunlit side only of the granulations. Now the white is "warmed" sufficiently that the artist must touch it with enough yellow to bring out the creaminess.

The tree shadows are blue. If you look at the cobalt sky of a winter's day, then quickly back to a large patch of shadow, that patch appears dark grey. But concentrate on that shadow and you know it is blue, but quite a different blue from the sky, more indigo, more purplish, but still intensely blue. The warmer the weather, the stronger these colours are.

When the morning and evening lights strike, the snow is tinted with rose and pale yellow and light purple, but now the shadows become deep lavender.

Snowscapes are not easy for the artist, and he must study his subject; the way the drifts lie, the way the wind sculptures them; the pattern of the ripples; the little hollows at the base of each wind-agitated twig or seed stalk; the tracks of animals and birds. All this and more you must notice, and then you see why snow is one of the most elusive things in all nature to portray. It is at once solid yet semi-liquid. Under the wind it can flow almost like water, yet it will pack into a drift upon which you can stand. Let it thaw at the surface, and it lies glazed and ready to reflect the sky and the trees. A fresh fall looks woolly and unbelievably soft, yet with the first wind the whole scene will change; the cotton-wool substance changes its nature, and will whirl and hiss from rooftops and trees to join with the ground blizzard which sends it skidding over the crust of earlier layers, and it does not sink to rest until it finds a windless spot in the lee of a barn or a patch of willows or a coulee bank.

And, separated from the mass, one flake of this elusive substance holds all the silver beauty of Canadian winter.

Snow serves both man and beast.

Should your soft-water tank fail, there is always the snow to be brought in and melted. Snow water is unbelievably soft; it caresses the skin, and women love it for hair washing. But if you like a good kitchen cup of tea, don't use snow water, for the resultant brew will be flat and flavourless. Tea seems to require a little mineral to bring out its goodness.

I said a kitchen cup, because camp tea is another story. That must needs be made with snow, but the trail "boil up" is made by letting the billycan come to the boil on your campfire, and just as it starts to bubble over, you throw a handful of tea into the hissing mass. Let it boil for about a minute, then take off the can and throw in a handful of sugar and stir vigorously with a stick. You will have a strong, sweet, satisfying drink which will take you many miles. But it doesn't taste right in a teacup. And, come to think of it, the nicer the cup is (I like a thin flowered one), the better your home tea tastes. Any old tin mug in the bush; but no thick, white, cheap-restaurant-style cup indoors, please.

After lakes, creeks, and springs freeze over, all wild creatures obtain their water requirements from snow. Most domestic stock can do the same. Horses running at large take to eating snow naturally, and although cattlemen generally feel their cattle should have water, I never bothered about it for range cattle in the Peace River foothills. Animals meeting their requirements for liquid this way take their snow little and often, which seems natural, for most fodder—hay, bundles of straw—is dry. I know that my cattle never humped up or stood shivering, as they usually do when they fill up once a day at a trough of cold water. Our fowls, too, in their log-and-dugout shed, looked forward to their daily pan of soft snow, pecking into it with clucks of approval.

Snow was used a great deal in earlier days. Even city people used to melt it, before everyone had a tap. On the farms there was often a shortage of water, and one of the daily chores for boys and girls used to be to fill one or more barrels with snow.

The barrels commonly lived behind the big cookstove, and the boys filled them from washtubs which had themselves been filled by scooping up the snow with a tin plate. If the snow was fresh-fallen and soft it took a lot to make a pail of water, and younger fry were employed by the older children to tramp the snow in the tub with their feet. Thus do we early learn to "exploit" the weaker; or, to put it a better way, thus do the young learn responsibility and obedience!

The melted snow was used for almost everything, and quite often if the well went dry or froze up, the work oxen or horses would be watered at the kitchen door in a washtub. Animals and men shared their surroundings much more in early days. While we didn't keep the pig in the parlour, nevertheless there were many calves, lambs, piglets, and baby chicks that Mother had to wrap in flannel and put by, or even within, the oven—to the delight of the children.

Even stabled horses would winter quite well if their owner shovelled the mangers full of snow once a day. A man might not grumble at a dried-up well, but he really had something to say if his snowdrift "played out on him."

In seeking to improve stock culture we sometimes forget that animals were able to live long before we domesticated them, and quite often we go to needless trouble. The earlier settlers from Europe were much concerned for their horses and cattle when they first encountered the prairie winter. Every animal, they thought, must be housed, and well housed. These people would stuff up every crack in a stable, and when the door was opened in the morning a great cloud of steam would rush out. Then when the animals were let out for water they suddenly met temperatures down to forty degrees below zero. The sudden transition was much harder on them than if the barn had been cool. Nature provides cattle and horses with a thick winter coat, and these animals can winter outside perfectly well, provided there is a patch of scrub or a creek bank or coulee where they can shelter from the bitter wind. Of course, horses at work which might cause them to sweat, or milch cows, which might freeze their teats, are quite a different matter.

Animals which "winter-kill" on the range very seldom die from the actual cold, but rather from starvation. Hunger may force them from shelter during a blizzard; they are not able to work through the crusted snow for grass, and wander or are swept onward before the wind till, unable to keep up their body heat, they give up the struggle.

The dreadful plight of the British cavalry horses in the Crimea was the result of stupidity on the part of hidebound commanders. The cavalry had always depended on fodder rather than grazing, and horse rations were laid down in the books at so many pounds of good timothy hay and so many pounds of oats. But the transports to the Crimea were seriously delayed, and the rations did not reach the horse lines where the wretched beasts were kept tied in shivering rows.

Yet all the time the Cossack cavalry were operating as usual. They had not lost touch with nature, and knew how to use her bounty. They wasted no time in providing their horses with what lay all around; their mounts were herded in loose bands by night, and they rustled the good steppe grass and ate the snow.

Much the same situation worked in favour of the Transvaal Boers, whose mobile, self-sufficient cavalry enabled their army to stay in the field so long. Had our military authorities thrown away their textbooks and taken a look at their surroundings, much suffering would have been avoided.

To the prairie chickens the snow is a downy sleeping bag. These birds burrow down in the drifts at night, and during prolonged storms they may stay snug and drifted over for several days, not venturing forth from their igloos till the wind drops.

The blizzards which at this season sweep across Saskatchewan come mostly on the heels of a northwest wind. They are bred in the realms of Keewadin and up the Mackenzie and in the Northern Peace River, commonly beginning as a heavy snowfall accompanied by rising temperatures.

But as they work south and east the winds increase until by the time the storm reaches the open prairie a real blizzard is in full cry, and the temperature will drop until the snowflakes become small, fine, sharp as sand, cutting the face like needles. It may blow for a day, or for six or seven. The driven snow which blots out the landscape is not all from the skies, for the cutting edge of sharp particles begins to erode the smooth billowing snowdrifts, hard-packed though they are. Soon, these begin to move, adding tons to what is falling from the skies. And so the blizzard goes, "dreeing its weird" across the landscape, picking up the snow, driving it, tossing it high, switching it like a whiplash around corners, dropping it like a threshing snake to coil about the edges of groves.

It is well to stay under cover, to hibernate. The blizzard will blow itself out, the eldritch gusts will be silent. Patience is the way of wild things, softly is the way of the countryman. Many lives have been lost. Many more will be, for some are dedicated and must be out—doctors and nurses and patrolmen. And many are foolhardy, forgetting that nature is still stronger than the clever inventions of man. We must come to terms with that.

When it is over, a calm falls. The sun comes up, pale, yellow, cold, but promising, asking us only to have patience yet a little while. On either side are his attendant "dogs"—those pale, eerie, watery reflections of his glory. The snowy hills to the east are as clear-cut and blue as glaciers. Distant sounds seem close. We hear a man's footsteps crunch in the snow half a mile away. We hear the clatter of his milk pail and the squeak of his barn door. His dog barks, and we can almost hear his indrawn breath, as we hear the husky indrawing of a rooster's after his crow. Every time I wake to a morning like this, I think of a bishop I heard of— I think he was the Bishop of Bloemfontein—who used to open his window, put out his head, and say: "Good morning, God!" A new day—that never was before! That bears no stain from yesterday, no sorrow, no despair. All that was cancelled by the soft, kindly night, the forgiving darkness.

A tree cracks, and it sounds like a rifle shot. We finish our coffee and go outside to assess the situation. At the southeast corner of each building is a great new drift, firmly packed. The ditches are full, the drifts waist deep, dusted with grit from the summer fallow, for on the smooth cultivated land there is little anchorage, and the wind has swept bare the knolls, sending dirt and snow scudding along together. When the snow melts in spring you will see the dust of the fallow lying among the dry weeds and grass of the roadside.

Wherever there stands a patch of willows or a few poplars in the fenceline, there will also be a drift, sometimes pointing a long finger right across the road, which is otherwise swept bare as if by a broom. Later we shall be able to gauge the height of the drift when we see, perhaps four or five feet from the ground, the twigs cut off sharply by the foraging rabbits, or the bark gnawed from the trees. Farmers have a busy day. Barn doors may have to be shovelled out, wells rediscovered among those cold dunes.

The sun is friendly at noon. He shines in at the window and warms the desk top. But for all the still brightness there is little warmth outside. The crisp cold overcomes him, and by night the thermometer will drop to thirty below, perhaps forty below or even lower. We say of old: "As the days lengthen the cold will strengthen." But the Spring Equinox does not seem so far away as it did, and, for all the cold, we have it on the tip of our tongues to say: "The back of winter is broken."

The boys' hands itch for their hockey sticks, their feet for the gleaming skates, and here, sure enough, comes Jim with his blade to clear the deep snow from the open-air rink.

We are rather proud of our winter!

If Janus is two-headed and looks both backward and forward, we can only say of February that she changes her mood with all the inconstancy of a wife or sweetheart. For this is also the month of February thaws, those unexpected glimpses of the promise of spring-to-come. It is during these mild spells that we realize that in the slowly mounting sun there is again some warmth. The days lengthen so gradually that we hardly notice the change, till one day as we switch on the lights we see by the clock that it is actually after five o'clock. In the milder air, in the absence of the earlier frost haze, we notice new colour creeping into the landscape. The poplar trunks show a touch of pale emerald, and the willow bark makes splashes of wine-red and purplish brown around the snow-filled sloughs.

In the thickets, the slender curved twigs of red osier dogwood are a rich rose-madder, while the rose hips, shrivelled though they are, glow dull orange and vermilion. The pendant clumps of winged seeds which hang from the ash and maple are ochre and Naples yellow. The clusters are more ragged now, for the evening grosbeaks have been at them.

These bold birds, with great conical, leaden beaks, are even now engaged in foraging for his favourite dainty. There a male, in black, white, and lemon yellow, drops the husk, even as his dove-grey mate leans far down, parrot-like, from her twig. She stretches full length, snatches a crisp winged seed from a bunch below, and, recovering, opens the packet with one clever crunch, and we see the twin wings, like those of an insect, float slowly downward. Where these birds have fed long, we see the hanging, denuded stalks only. The fruit is gone. And soon the birds themselves will wing their chirruping way to other trees, other villages, other barnyards. They do not, as a rule, stay long in one place. Neither do the Bohemian waxwings which we see on any berry bush, but more especially on their favourite buffalo berry, picking the dried, dull-red fruit from among the wicked thorns. See how they desist from the feast to hop and flutter to the topmost branches, there to sun themselves and preen their silky plumage, raising and lowering their neatly pointed crests. They seem to converse gently among themselves in softly trilling waxwing language.

On these milder days the chickadees find a new note which pleases their ears greatly, and ours not a little. They greet us with a double note, not in the hurried way they usually talk, but in a slow, easy, and musical whistle. So clearly is it uttered that we cannot but sense the message. The Crees say the birds are telling us of spring. *Nee-pin* is their word for that season, and *nee-pin* is what those notes sound like, though white children translate it "Spring's here!"

But spring is not as close as that. Any day now we may see that deceitful glow of duck-egg green in the northwest. Behind that, always, lies another blizzard.

In the meantime we enjoy the thaw.

Early in the morning, just before and at the time of the sun's rising, we may, if we have a wide enough view, see the beauty of the winter mirage, as warmed air rises from the snowfields. We see the elevators of distant towns painted above the horizon; we see knolls become mountains and coulees assume the form of great, shadowed canyons; we see clumps of trees changed into the likeness of turreted castles. By noon these have vanished. The dream is over, the fairy landscape lies again flat to the horizon. But now, in the sun's warmth, we faintly smell the barnyards and the stables. The sweet odour of hay, of straw, of dung, strikes us the more strongly, and is all the more savoury because throughout the sub-zero weather it has been locked in the frost. And during the noon hours we hear the soft drip of water from the roof, and notice how the snow is shrinking away from the south side of tree trunks and fenceposts.

As the sun sets, the air cools again, the surface of the snow hardens, the footsteps of passers-by crackle, and the drip from the eaves freezes and gradually solidifies into long tapered icicles as big as carrots.

We have always enjoyed the long winter evenings at this time of year.

So many books are available, and we are able to get through those we buy, as well as those sent us from the East and from England. We always get a winter parcel of them from the Victoria League in London, which are the best of travel, history, and biography from all over the Commonwealth. This year we have read several more on the new Africa. One of these, *Drawn in Colour* by Noni Jabavu, is really outstanding. She is a highly educated Xhosa woman of the transkei who really loves her country—Boers, Britons, and all—and ends her book, typically, with an old Taal saying: *"Alles sal rag kom"*—all will come right.

With real regret we close her book and put it on the shelf marked "Africa," along with *Red Strangers, A Thing to Love, Cry, the Beloved Country,* and *Turning Wheels.*

The culture of Noni's people, like that of Van der Post's bushman, is the culture of a country people from which we may learn much wisdom. These people, like many of us, live on great open plains, and have had to come to terms with scanty rainfall.

By way of contrast we turn to more involved matters in our old favourite books by Kipling and Tolstoy, Conrad and the Sitwells—Osbert and Sacheverell—and we see how closely linked are all these writers, Bantu and Russian, Polish and English, in their common understanding of humanity and environment.

The tales told by the smoky dun fires of the African dusk are a people's story. They have a directness of approach and an innate sense of rightness which are often obscured in our writings and our thoughts by the multiplicity of divisions by which we approach our subject. Instinctual understanding and rational contemplation, practicality and theory, emotion and grace, are rarely brought together, and the natural world appears either a scientific arrangement of cold facts, or an unfortunate accident, or a sentimental and only half-seen world of pretty butterflies—none of which have much to do with our personal lives. Only when Science and the Humanities are properly welded together shall we ever be able to present, as does the Bantu, one whole world. And we must only *apply* science in the light of this wholeness of matter and spirit, facts and faith.

Much as we detest the use of radio for crying the wares of the commercial world, we have to admit that this invention makes available a great deal of the good music we are privileged to hear, and, much as we may disagree with many of the Canadian

Broadcasting Corporation programmes, we are nevertheless grateful to that body.

Unfortunately, so many speakers who are interviewed express opinions based on little knowledge. This is especially true of groups (non-professional) who discuss this and that. The danger is that there is no moderator to gather up the various remarks and straighten them out, and as a result many people think that because these people are heard on the air they are knowledgeable and worth listening to.

We look forward to weekday evenings when we hear Beethoven and Bach and Handel. One unforgettable time we heard Dale Bartlett play the *Sonata Apassionata,* and I was confronted by my boyhood with my mother at the piano. Such lovely pieces moved me greatly then, as now; later I was to hum snatches of this music on many a lonely trail, and recall it at many a campfire with sweet nostalgia.

When wearied from long reading, we wander out to do our shopping. We enjoy the change from the written to the spoken word as we join in the chat of the village store.

Better still, I stroll down to George's garage. Here a sort of a loose men-only club gathers. We do not meet by any prearrangement, but rather by the accident of mutual desire to see who is around and what they know today. We sit where we can, on upturned buckets or boxes, enjoying the heat of the old-fashioned coal stove. Pipes are filled, cigarettes rolled, matches struck, as one subject after the other is picked up, commented on, and dropped. Several are old soldiers, and we hear the words Loos and Vimy and Cambrai, or memories of the Menin Road and Passchendale. It seems like a dream now—the mud, the desolation, and the heights to which men can rise. Juniper Junction may, to a stranger, appear backward—a hick place—but the affairs of the nation receive very careful consideration in all the little Juniper Junctions from sea to sea. The approach is nothing if not direct, and yet in the simplest words there is the deep, natural philosophy of the countryman.

One says of modern concepts, modern education: "Oh well, you know, they say if you can't beat them, join them." But he is assailed from all sides. He tries another tack, and he comes back with: "Who wants to be called an oddball?" Everyone laughs, but you know that deep down they are content to be oddballs, "squares" as the children say. They will be more careful how they express themselves when they go home.

George himself comes and goes at his work, or pops his head in from the cluttered shop behind the office, perhaps to ask someone for a hand at shifting some heavy piece—and the help is freely forthcoming.

All the time he munches peanuts, till you wonder how the monkeys in the zoo are going to fare. His addiction goes back to the days he quit smoking—which he did for a very good reason. He has a fine tenor voice, and if he should miss a church service you know at once that George is not there.

His establishment is not architecturally up to date. It looks like an old blacksmith shop, but George has a real knack with stubborn motors and it is said of him that "what he can't fix he'll make."

This, then, is our village forum in the best traditions of pre-Roman Britain; our pub-without-beer.

This apparently sleeping village is far from being so in fact. In the sense that it is quiet and sober, there is that peaceful atmosphere we may equate with sleepiness. But that atmosphere results from the fact that our settlers were well-bred and well-brought-up people in the first place; country people of sound rural values, unaccustomed to strife, petty jealousy, or disregard for law and order. None of the "Smart Yankee" types, so many of whom came across our borders for the good (as Mrs. Moody wrote in *Roughing It in the Bush* in 1838) "of their own country" ever obtained a foothold here.

On the last day of February we walked down the railway track. Passing a bluff in the adjoining field, we noticed that someone had been cutting green poles. On the way back we detoured, following a hard-packed rabbit trail. The sun was setting, painting the sky all red behind the stark poplar trunks. As we entered the bluff a dark shape fled before us. It was a goshawk, and soon we found a little patch of red in the snow and then a little pile of blue-white fur that had been a rabbit.

Such places are real traps for the little snowshoes, for the woodcutters lop the limbs from the poles, piling them to one side, and the rabbits are attracted to them for the sweet bark of the terminal twigs. The snow was hard-packed by their splay-toed, furry feet, and the nanny berries lay everywhere. Most of the branches were gnawed bare of the grey-green bark. But their feast had not gone unnoticed by the red-eyed hawk.

At the bird's approach, the group reaction we call panic must have seized the furry folk. Only one was too late, as one must always be. Pan gives warning indeed, but Pan is responsible for hawks as well as rabbits; and in all this, terrible and bloody as the individual acts of survival must be, there is no malice, and nature remains innocent.

Luckily these birds of prey only visit the settlements in winter, preferring to breed and raise their young in the green and tangled sanctuary of the North Woods.

CHAPTER XII

March—The Moon of Light

February has passed away.

It gave us blizzards and thaws, and now March comes in like a lamb, but he will change his shape and roar before the month is out. This fake spring of the past two days has brought out a few pussy willows, but they are foredoomed; and the longer days have brought into blossom more than these innocent furry flowers.

Early in March we were visited by the Mounted Policeman from Lumsden. He asked if we could identify some stolen property, supposedly taken during a break-in at Pelican Point in which our cottage was involved.

There was an old buffalo gun of mine (a present from a long-dead old-timer), a Mexican sombrero from Chihuahua, a moosehide coat made for me by Katchik's squaw in my northern days, and a sword from Borneo, which was especially precious to me. It was a head-hunter's weapon, and had been brought to England a hundred and forty years ago by a great-uncle in the British Navy. It used to hang in my father's studio. Alas! This priceless piece had been sadly used. The lovely bead-and-cowrie-shell scabbard had been stripped off, and the intricately carved ivory hilt with its plumes of hair and tusked demon head was smashed. It had been used to break windows in effecting entry to other cottages.

These were part of the useless loot taken by three juveniles from the city. We went out to survey the damage. Nothing else was taken, but books had been torn from the shelves and thrown face-downward open on the floor, pages mutilated and dirtied. Books, many of them irreplaceable, books which to these youths represented a world to which they had never been introduced, which they would never know, in spite of the thousands of dollars spent on them by the Government.

Pictures had been torn from walls, stepped on by muddy feet, and their frames broken. Chests of manuscripts and drawings—the observations of years—had been emptied, and their contents scattered. Some of these papers had been used to light the stove, although there were newspapers in plenty. Mud and filth were everywhere.

What did these products of our way of life think they would find in a cottage? Money? Perhaps I should have left some bills on the table as a bribe. The loss would have been much less. They had broken a back window to get in, and through this, after their departure, the snow had drifted and half melted, then turned to ice at night. I could not but remember the early days of homesteading and pioneering when a man could leave a wagon by the roadside, a canoe by a river, or a saddle hung in a tree in the certainty that in three months or three years he could return that way and find all as he left it, no matter how many had passed by in the meantime.

Daily the light grows.

What a wonderful thing is Light! Light of the sun, light of the mind!

Last week we went to Regina. As we approached in the March dusk a light rose slowly above the curving plain; up, up, till we could see, in illuminated glory, the whole towering bulk of the Saskatchewan Power Building. Brand-new, sheathed in shining metal and glass, it sends its beams across the flat prairie in beckoning welcome.

The greatest achievement yet, the symbol of man's needs fulfilled—so the papers had said at the opening a year ago. And I thought of the pomp and circumstance of that opening, which we had attended. Certainly no one can deny the benefits of electric power, and no one wishes to. The High Priests, the potentates, of this temple of light deserved, I am sure, the plaudits accorded them.

The streets had buzzed with talk. Yes, we agreed, man's ingenuity had brought light to every prairie hamlet, every isolated farmhouse. Yes, we have achieved a New Freedom, and this temple was the outward, glorious manifestation which from now on would be pointed out to every visitor, to every tourist. Now, indeed, the prairie blossomed where once the bones of bison rotted in the grass!

But squatting in the shade of this great temple, squatting like a beggar woman on the steps of Santa Rita in Chihuahua, we see another building, small, drab, its old bricks lichened, grey and whitewashed by the brown sparrows, the avian beggars which gather by night in the shelter of its eaves and porch. It is a little Catholic church. It has stood on this corner since Regina was a bustling, muddy frontier town. From a common—perhaps instinctive—impulse we enter. The door does not open on our approach, it is activated by no seeing eye. We have to lift the latch and push, and as the door opens, the hinges squeak slightly, just enough to tell us that they were not hung yesterday.

It is dusty within, and we grope for a pew. No air conditioner ruffles our hair, no hum of electrical heating throbs in our ears; our footsteps sound eerily like those of lost people.

And then, ahead, we see a little gleam of ruby red, above where we know the altar to be. It does not force itself upon us. It is just there, flickering slightly.

It is the sanctuary lamp that no power failure can put out, for it is not controlled by switches or fed by wires. It is apart, itself, benign, beneficent, beatifying. Loving hands keep the oil at level, loving hands tend this tiny flame which glows amidst the faint sweet smell of incense, symbolizing the Light of the World.

The things of man are good. The things of God are better. We are reminded of those who said: *"Aha! We are warm, we have seen the fire, to deliver us. We waited for light . . . but we walk in darkness till we follow the righteousness of Jerusalem, which goes forth as a lamp and a brightness."*

Now we know we stand in the presence of the source of all light. The Light which came into the world for all men; the Light which lit the very brain of man, that he might see to harness the great mysterious forces of nature from which the illumination next door owes its being. If, in the harnessing and the putting to use, man forgot the source, that is his loss. The light at the altar is the only light which can lead from delinquency to freedom.

But there is a natural darkness, too, in our world, and that is blessed because in it we have trust. A man I knew, who had spent many years in the Arctic, told me that the season of the midnight sun was the hardest to bear, for then he felt naked and exposed and longed for a soft darkness. Man as yet cannot bear this nakedness. At times he must hide; he must burrow.

The Light which shone on the Damascus road was brief and merciful. Softly, easily, is the way of God—and nature.

We cannot all be aware of God in the same way that St. Paul was. The world puts up too many barriers, and so many do not understand, even after two thousand years. The worst disservice the reformers did to religion was throwing away the Catechism and substituting a moral code based on ethics, respectability, and acceptance by a group. At least this is what it looked like to many people. Ever since then the majority of people have not understood the doctrine of original sin. They get it mixed up with sex. The Catechism explained man's relationship to God in a manner no Sunday-school books could ever do, and that is what the business of Christianity is about. Religion is not so much a matter of being "nice" or "horrid" as being aware of God. Of knowing the Light. *Et lux tenebris erat, et tenebrae eam non comprehenderunt.*

The seventeenth, the day of Ireland, comes and goes. St. Patrick, the shamrock, the bottle-green coat, the cudgel and the hat; these, to the Anglo-Saxon, are still the Hibernian tradition. The tradition of a people who charm us with their music and their mixture of smiles and tears, yet who so often exasperate us. After so many attempts to make amends, we are still cudgelled, we who neither wished for nor engineered a famine in their "pratie fields."

Only five days now to the Equinox.

We have had fierce winds, and winter shows no signs of its old age; but surely, steadily, the sun extends his daily visits, and we begin to be impatient.

We had been tramping through the snow to watch some newly returned horned larks. These are among the very first birds to wing their way from the south. Not that all of them have so far to come, for many larks winter on the High Plains of the Missouri Coteau, which is not so far distant as birds fly.

This morning we heard their thin, wiry notes overhead, and then saw a little flock settle on the road. We followed them, and found more at the edge of a stubble field, feeding on weed tops above the snow. Hard by was a flock of snow buntings, still in the pink-washed plumage of winter, which will fade to immaculate black and white within a month, when they will be gathering for the northward flight to their soggy tundras. Up to now these had been the chief of the seed gleaners, together with a few chirpy redpolls. The horned larks look much larger, and their soft pinkish-gray colouring makes them harder to see among the withered stalks. Their tails are dark, however, and although these are concealed almost to the tip by the tail coverts, they show up strongly when spread in flight.

The drifts were deep. They would almost bear our weight, they were so packed. But not quite; for at each step, after a brief pause, one's foot went through.

We turned for home. The setting sun made a red streak above the horizon, and the rolling prairie lay smoky blue, and so other-worldly that we could not imagine it would ever again become lush, green, and bearing. So the moon will look when man first breaks her silence with his impious step.

I was sweating, and the chill wind of evening made me shiver.

It was in the east. Curious how the east wind has always been cursed by man! (I remember it at Scarborough, by the North Sea. "Bracing!" my uncle said it was, and I as a small boy thought that bracing was not quite a nice word!) Next morning I woke with a sharp pain in my chest. I got up as usual, but the pain increased and I went back to bed. Hope telephoned to Regina for a doctor, who said he would drive out.

During my convalescence a funeral was held in the village. As I watched the sombre yet glossy hearse go by, I could see inside it the costly coffin and all the trimmings. I thought, what a pity these things could not be simple. Why should status symbols enter into such proceedings? The widow is deprived of her rights. Traditionally, men stood aside at such times, and it was the wifely privilege to fold the hands, draw down the eyelids, and pass the winding sheet around. Now she is cheated. She has no such work to ease her heart. She is hardly allowed to let the tears flow, and few weep with her to ease the ache of loss. Rather, she must be "taken out of herself." They say: "Don't cry so, you'll make yourself ill." She will be far more ill for denying nature. Better to say: "Sister, see? We weep with you," as the Indian women do, for, as they say: "In three days comes peace."

We are far too embarrassed in the face of death and of sorrow. Why do we say: "I was shocked to hear . . ."? Why be shocked at what is as natural and inevitable as birth? I would prefer to die in bed, with Hope's hand in mine. I would prefer that she performed the last offices. I would prefer a shroud to a coffin.

And at the last I do not want my widow to be presented with an enormous bill; but the world of commerce must have its tribute, and society would look askance at such a simple arrangement. There is but one thing to fear after all. Only those who live without God will die without Him.

I was getting about again. At dusk I could hear the horned owls at their courting. This is not the hollow *hoo! hoo!* we have heard all winter, but a mixture of soft notes mixed with blood-curdling howls and screeches. One feels that their lovemaking must be like that of tigers—as fierce, as primeval in its vocal expression.

They will choose for their nesting place the abandoned nest of a crow or a large hawk, for the owls are not builders in their own right. The big white eggs will be well screened from view at this height, and the fierce-eyed owlets will live on that flattened, twiggy platform until they are as large as their parents. It will take many rabbits and mice to keep their cavernous mouths content; but soon the crows will be back, and until the leaves open these dusky carrion birds will be the owls' for the taking, for the crows must roost in the naked trees.

Once, later, some boys dislodged a young owl from its nest by using a long pole. The bird was almost fully grown as to size, but still in the down, through which the pin feathers showed blue. The creature fell, clutching at the branches with its long curved talons, finally securing a hold about six feet above the ground, and there it remained, talons locked. Hanging upside down, it twisted its head about, glaring horribly. The boys tried to capture him, but his snapping bill, his awful hisses and his death grip on the branch were too much for them and they beat a retreat. He hung thus till next day, when I finally released that bulldog grip, and he flopped to the rustling leaves below. Regaining an upright posture, he spread his pinionless wings and defied me with the ferocity of a great cat. I wished him well and left him.

We heard the first crow on March 28. Next day a small bunch of perhaps a dozen appeared, winging their way in that desultory flight which rises and falls over the fields and misses nothing edible. Their caws at this time have not quite the hoarse, raucous quality of fall. These early spring notes have a milder, almost a tired sound. After all, they have come from far and may be weary, if no less wary than when we said goodbye in October. On a warm day one or another may delight us with a gentle mating call—*k-o-lio!*—which few people realise crows are capable of.

But this is not spring.

There must come, as every countryman knows, the Storm of Crows—the snowfall (and perhaps blizzard) which strikes once, at least, after the first black scouting parties have appeared to spy out the land with hoarse complaints. When that storm came it was a rough one, dumping several inches of snow so white that the partly thawed drifts of winter looked dirty by comparison. The wind swept the new snow across the old, and made fresh, soft mounds in new places, for this storm came from the east.

When it was over it turned clear and frosty. The sun was now high at its meridian, and the glare of new snow made the eyes ache. This is the month when snow blindness can strike at its worst. With modern transportation this affliction has become uncommon, but I have had at least two painful attacks in years gone by. On horseback it is not so bad, one can look down at the horse's neck and the saddle, but on snowshoes there is little between one and the glare, and our only protection was to smear our noses with lampblack and lard.

The storm has taken its toll. Under the wooden sidewalks, in the lee of stacks, and around the thin shelter of farm implements, we found the bodies of many dead horned larks. We found a few not quite dead, and we brought these to the kitchen, but we could not keep them more than one night, for those which recovered could have beaten themselves to death in their box.

They too have the right to die peacefully on the prairie, and not be intruded upon.

We let them out into the care of the wilderness, and that night the frost lessened.

We were on the doorstep of April.

CHAPTER XIII

April—The Moon of Spring

The sap is fairly leaping now. We see it in the deepening colour of bark in the bluffs and bushes. We see it in the more erect carriage and the quicker movements of old people, and it fairly bubbles over in the young. For the sap of spring runs through bones and flesh as well as up the trunks of trees and vines.

No need now to watch your step to avoid icy patches, or bumps, or hollows in the beaten snow. We can lift our eyes from the way we travel and, once more, allow them to seek the sky tints of the horizon. We are free, released from the thralldom of winter which has hitherto circumscribed our feet, our eyes, and our activities.

The cattle, newly released to the open stubble lands and pastures of dry, snow-flattened grass, leap and play, or just stand soaking in the warm sunshine. But the very warmth thus engendered has a debilitating effect on the newly freed beasts. They have been so long accustomed to eating enormously in order to build up body heat against the cold that it seems that their appetites have now become more fickle. They smell spring, they smell the promise of new verdue, and they are seized with strange restlessness. But they smell only the promise, for the fulfillment is still some weeks away.

Their heat, coming now from the outside, serves only to shrink them. The meat on their ribs becomes flaccid, their hips look wasted, there are deep hollows in their flanks. An old cattleman will tell you that now they are at their weakest, that on the range older cows which have "toughed it" through the bitter months of winter in good shape may, with hope within their grasp, simply and suddenly give up and die. April is actually one of the worst months for losses. A cold, bitter spring storm can kill more cattle than the worst that winter can offer.

It is as if the beasts had fought for life too long, as if hope deferred had so exhausted the fighting spirit that they give up without a struggle.

Many farmers and some ranchers like to have a few acres of crested wheat grass for this season. The grass, imported from Asia, was widely sown by the the P.F.R.A. in its programme of reseeding submarginal and abandoned land following the Depression years. As soon as the snow goes, this hardy plant will send up a multitude of young shoots, and such a greensward provides that early bite which is a lifesaver to cattle, for the native grasses respond more slowly to spring's urge. It is all a matter of vitamin A and chlorophyll, this sudden languor which besets the beasts.

To increase the ration of forage feeds—hay, straw or bundles, or even whole grain or chop—does not help much. The cattle have not the appetite, and on a warm spring day will trample and spoil more than they eat. They need something else, and they will stand and gaze, snuffing the air and lowing.

The cows which have been delivered, who have crept off to calve and are now licking dry the velvety coats of their young, are even more hollow-flanked, but now they have a purpose in life, and their eyes are brighter for it. They are prepared to eat everything, for now they must make milk. They are lighter by many pounds and graze hurriedly, cropping the old grass fast but not steadily, for between tufts they keep glancing towards the patches of low bush and tangled weeds which shelter their unseen and unmoving calves.

The snow is melting madly. What was so white and dead seems to have come to joyous life and, in sympathy with the upward-pushing sap, now moves from the exposed slopes, at first sluggishly; warily, too, as if timid and unsure of its new-found fluidity, its new mobility, seeping rather than running.

The surface, honeycombed by the day's wind and sun, crystallizes anew by night, so that in early morning it appears glassy and shot with mother-of-pearl. During the day the water drains slowly through its mass to the frozen ground beneath; and there is a secrecy in this, for we hardly realise that thawing is in progress at all till we note the widening circles of dark, soggy grass about each rock, each clump of brush, whose darker colours have absorbed the sun's rays and thus heightened the immediate temperature. Sometimes, even as we look at an expanse of deep snow which has been thus undermined, we hear a soft "Woosh!" and see the whole surface collapse six inches or a foot, and then we see the dark water itself, perhaps an inch deep, in spots where the collapse was complete and the upper surface has drowned itself.

A few really warm days complete the disintegration, but there remain still large shallow pools, waiting for the push of gravity to unlock the damming drifts; when suddenly, as a passage is forced, the whole mass of leaden, lifeless liquid is quickened, and rushes down the several declivities which have for centuries guided the transformed snows of winter to the lower ground. Every slough fills with the cold flood unable to escape further, since there are no outlets from these saucer-like depressions which dimple the plains. Should there be, then the pool is no slough, but merely the widening of a draw which will mark the head of a coulee. And it is down these coulees or ravines that the released waters soon leap and froth, gathering dry trash to weave among the willows and rose bushes, looking like worn-out mats or birds' nests. The water in its wake leaves the long grass dankly plastered down, like a woman's new-washed hair.

So runs the snow water—breathless, eager, dreaming of its tryst with the looping, winding creeks, and later the mighty rivers which will join this soft brown flood with bitter, ice-green waters of Hudson's Bay.

Stand above the bank of a darkly wooded coulee on an April night, and if your thoughts are not tuned that-a-way, if you do not feel the mystery and the charm and the longing of this hurry and bustle, then probably you will not notice the little saw-whet owl which at this season sharpens his steel all night—*whitsa-whitsa-whitsa.* He stops for a brief interlude, and he will move his perch among the budding trees, for when next he picks up his refrain it will be to one side or the other. He does not cease till daylight, and we hope his patience will soon be rewarded, and a little hen owl will fly to him.

Spring winds are harsh in Saskatchewan, yet the buds swell a little each day, and they are worthy of a close look. Seen against the sky, the shapes show up specifically, clear-cut, allowing of no confusion. White poplar buds alternate on the main twig, bunched at the end, round and sharply pointed. Maple buds, the loveliest of all, clasping and opposite, with the terminal bud the finest shaped, geometrically designed, coloured in soft mauve with a grape-like bloom; these have a sculptured, classical beauty to delight the artist's eye.

The willows, again, bear alternate buds, rich and glossy as the coat of a chestnut horse. Soon they will break into pussy mittens, all silky grey dusted with gold.

Black poplar is our common name for *Populus balsamfora,* but earlier settlers—lovers of Biblical phraseology—called this tree balm of Gilead, a much more romantic name, but often shortened to "balm." The name is a descriptive one, for this tree carries large, shining buds, strongly aromatic and as sticky as sugarplums. These trees are not so common here as in the North, nor do they attain the great height and girth that we see along the North Saskatchewan River. Their trunks are greener than those of white poplar (*Populus tremeloides*) or quaking asp, and in the older trees the bark is rugose and deeply cleft.

On our Peace River ranch we had several of these enormous old trees overshadowing the house, and in a heavy spring wind the buds used to fall in our rain-water barrels. A friend visiting from England used to dip her jug into the soft water preparatory to her morning ablutions. So intrigued was she with the fragrance added to the water by the "balm" buds that she insisted on picking several handfuls of them to take home. She wrote later from Sussex to say she had made up some sachets of them which she kept in her handkerchief drawer.

These buds are much beloved of all the grouse family, but especially ruffed grouse, and at this season we may see one or more of these birds climbing acrobatically among the terminal twigs in search of them.

The cold winds sweep across the open fields, drying the ground, and the damp grass which has lain flat so long under the weight of the snow now loses the ochre tint of its moist condition and bleaches almost to white. Nothing daunted, the anemones, true daughters of the wind, thrust their silky, stout buds above the ground, and soon the sunny sides of the knolls where the grass is short will be studded with the pale mauve flowers, delicate and papery. They are what we of the West call crocuses.

All this renewal of life—the cascading water, the song of the small owl, the opening of willow and crocus buds—is leading up to something grander and greater.

It is as if a young girl's flushed and happy face peered around her door, as if she said: "I'll be ready in a moment!" And you think, as she reappears: "Can this be my daughter? This creature with the gossamer frock and shining hair and the sudden new look of womanhood?"

It is Easter Day, and the fulfillment is here. The wind has softened. A robin has returned and is hopping across the lawn as if he had never left.

A bluebird, dark against the spring sky, flits down to the clothes-line, and suddenly, against the brushwood hedge of caragana, he is blue—intensely, violently blue.

A flicker is calling loudly from a nearby tree, and then you hear the tattoo of his stout bill as he sends his message vibrating through the village; the message that he is ready and waiting and has found a summer home. And we know that in some mysterious

way a lady flicker will respond and arrive on fluttering golden
wings. They will cross bills and talk a bit before they settle down.
With all our telephone and postal services we have not improved
so much on nature's ways; there is a Jack for every Jill and they
can communicate. They know many things we have forgotten,
and they are not subject to fear, that fear we have that we shall
be overlooked, forgotten. The prophet Jeremiah uses a wild thing
to illustrate this in the words: *"A wild ass, used to the wilderness,
that snuffeth up the wind at her pleasure; in her occasion who can
turn her away? All they that seek her shall not weary themselves;
in her month they shall find her."*

We gather at church, and we give collective thanks for the
renewal of life and, because we do not grow palm trees in
Saskatchewan, we like to call the pussy willows "palms" and
carry them in our hands, as the robed people of long ago carried
the green, fringed boughs, waving them beside and before the
humble donkey with its Burden.

We would waste less time, I think, in idle speculation as well
as in misdirected research and experiment, if we were more ready
to come to terms—or remain on terms—with nature and the
nature of man.

A few weeks ago Hope and I listened to a science professor
giving a radio talk on the possibilities of a future life—an eternal
life. The idea was that since it is a matter of certainty (!) that
in a few centuries science will be able to bring the dead to life,
we need not remain dead forever. All we need is to be deep-frozen
as soon as we die, then suitably stored to await the great day of
material resurrection.

If the good professor can convince enough people of the possibility of being awakened in years to come; if he can persuade
them of the desirability of being rudely reintroduced into a world,
presumably much changed, a world in which the individual will
have to be reindoctrinated and cultured by special schools—
then what a boon he has conferred upon the world of commerce!

Think of the money spent in labour and materials! Think of

the apparatus for freezing the dead! Think of the underground miles of chromium-lined mausoleums! Think of the bookwork, of the army of computers to record and to card-index the names and numbers! Think of the opportunities for revenge! Think of *Card 10899978—Symons, R. D. Due for resurrection 4500 A.D.* with CANCELLED stamped across it. Reference to file number will show cause: "He wrote against the scheme in 1965."

The burying and embalming professions are doing pretty well with our "remains" as it is, but what they now charge will be peanuts to the initial disposition costs of this system, let alone the rents which will be chargeable to several later generations. Good Brother Tetzel was a mere piker, and Longfellow's Cobbler of Hagenau would find his poor lady had only paid the first installment.

The new Tower of Babel flourishes. The confusion of tongues is immense. Already we are told we do not "relate," do not "communicate," those of us who speak simple Anglo-Saxon, who say *kill* for *harvest;* who see, instead of *having an awareness of;* do not define our terms when we use the ordinary speech which has served us so long.

Once the Western world thought the alphabet of twenty-six letters was an improvement over older methods of writing. Twenty-six simple letters which could be juggled to describe every thought, to name every creature and place. It was a marvel of simplicity. It did away with the long and weary process of memorizing thousands of phrases, expressions, and single words which were shown pictorially as in Chinese. Yet today our educators are abandoning simplicity. Our children must learn to recognise C-A-T as a word, rather than to know what to say if the positions of the letters are changed about.

Carried to extremes, this makes the dictionary useless, and may partly account for the meagre and narrow vocabulary of today's young people. They can only say a thing is good—not tasteful, charming, useful, delightful, convenient, well-formed, modest, amusing, or beautiful. "I'm doing good," says the boy who has passed his grade.

My mother, when she was a young married woman, was bicycling along a Sussex lane. She caught up to a flock of sheep being taken by their shepherd to another pasture. The lane being crowded from hedge to hedge, she slipped off her machine until the shepherd's dog, obedient to its master's signal, had made a passage. As she remounted and smilingly thanked the man, he removed his battered hat and, apparently addressing the flock, said: "Oh, the roses in her cheeks and her coal-black hair!"

He had no grade-twelve education. But he could express, quite spontaneously, poetry and chivalry and appreciation of beauty, all in the soft South Saxon tongue, kith and kin to the speech of Chaucer, Shakespeare, and Thomas Hardy.

On another occasion my mother's cook, having emptied down her throat the contents of a bottle of brandy intended for culinary use, had to be put to bed. Next morning my mother, faced with the unpleasant task of giving the woman notice, started off with: "Cook! You were disgracefully drunk last night."

"Drunk, ma'am?" replied the indignant cook. *"Drunk? What* a word for a young lady to use!"

Perhaps that was the beginning of today's habit of beating about the bush. From such reactions sprang our modern phraseology, which conceals all the implications of certain jobs under semi-professional names. Morticians, Geriatric Attendants, Rodent Control Officers, are examples that occur at once. All our geese must be swans and every bird stuffer a taxidermist, in the good cause of public relations and mental hygiene.

Romeo would not today be "in love." He would "have an emotional relationship" with Juliet. He would "equate her with good," while the Capulets and the Montagues would form a couple of "hate groups motivated by non-acceptance."

If mankind does its best to be sophisticated, to conceal so much beauty of thought and purpose beneath a veil of ugliness, to reduce dignity to vulgarity, to substitute knowledge for wisdom, the pursuit of pleasure for happiness; the world of nature continues its calm, even cycle and is not ashamed.

The world turns on its axis, the time is set by the heavenly bodies, the seasons complete their purpose, and in the words of Kipling *"the procession proceeds according to precedence."*

There is that perfect unity in diversity which we of the rubber-stamp era have lost sight of—to the imperilling of our noble confederation of provinces.

Let us then rejoice in the budding of the leaf, in the tinkle of water, and in the return of the birds, which never disappoint us.

The geese are thrusting north, the swans are again snow-white above the blue waters which divide the now rotten rafts of green ice drifting aimlessly to their consummation.

The army of shore birds gathers at the waterline, standing in rows as if, like Canute, they would forbid the waters to lap their scaled and gilded feet.

The wild drakes splash and quack, or pursue each other over reed beds—green heads, black heads, and russet heads—all among the mottled, sober-garbed ducks which are their wives.

Dusk and dawn are the times to be afoot by the waterside, in the thickets, or on the prairie knolls. Early this morning we drove into a large pasture where we had heard the clucking of sharp-tailed grouse the previous evening. Now we determined to watch the morning dance (or "display," as the biologists say).

A streak of light appears behind the low eastern hills, silhouetting their smooth crests above the level plain. An early breeze rustles through the short grass, brushing the faces of sleeping anemones.

The plains awake to life, not slowly as in more temperate and wooded climes, but suddenly. The sun, like a flaming disc, arises from behind the earth's curve. A meadow lark mounts a sprig of wolf willow to sing.

With a dry *whirr* a group of grouse rise from the prairie grass and rock on stiff wings to the top of a low knoll. For a moment they pick about aimlessly. Soon from far and wide come more grouse, in twos and threes, shattering the silence with their wings, *cuk-uking* throatily, landing on outthrust, feathered feet, running rapidly between the first comers. Now they stand, heads up, statuesque, gilded by the sun's first rays, their shadows long on the trampled knoll.

And now, far on the lonely prairie, as their ancestors have done, with no audience but the brown grass birds and the gophers, they solemnly begin sparring for partners. Pairing off, facing each other, the cock birds crouch with wings stiffly dragging and tails directed above their backs to show off the white fluffiness of undercoverts. Round and round, retreating and advancing, jumping simultaneously to meet in mid-air with a thud, only to spring apart and circle again, while the air is full of their throaty notes.

Bowing and scraping, showing off their crests, erecting their yellow eye combs, or suddenly whirling like tops with wings held stiff, their tramping feet producing a rattling sound which makes the very air vibrate.

They take time for breath, and squat for a minute, picking at the ground as if about to dust themselves, but spring to life again, distending their throat sacs to the likeness of purple plums, and recommence their chuckling and booming.

All the while more birds are arriving to join the lists, while others, wearying of the dance, leave their companions, to feed among the shrubbery. But not for long. Soon the laggards return and start again.

The bright-eyed ladies feed demurely, or simply watch, and soon it can be seen that certain cocks, more dominant than the rest, are taking charge of affairs.

So the tournament goes on, the clucking increases, and farm folk doing their morning chores say to one another: "Listen! Don't you hear the chickens dancing?"

Soon the shadows begin to shorten, and as if at a given signal the show breaks off. Plumage is smoothed down, heads raised to see that no danger lurks, bodies are briefly crouched, and by ones and threes and fives the birds launch themselves from the ground, and are soon lost in the folds of the plain.

A mottled feather floats slowly to the dance floor, already

trampled and feather-strewn. A gopher hurries by, intent on its business. The meadow lark sings again from his twig.

Otherwise the stage is empty, and we turn for home.

The Crees used to trap prairie chickens in horsehair snares at these dance grounds. In those days this did little harm to their numbers. The Indians also danced the "chicken dance" as a compliment to them. We do neither. But our motorcars and shot-guns, our bulldozers and road builders, are decimating these lovely creatures at a tragic rate.

Dawn and dusk. The owl and the grouse have their hours in the cycle of time and of days.

There is a deep significance for man in this, and in the move-ments of the heavenly bodies. Man has arisen to many dawns, and been overcome by many thick and impenetrable dusks.[1] Em-pires have risen and fallen. Times have been good and bad. We have had our cycles of success and failure, our ages of despair, and our Golden Ages. So it will ever be.

But always, during the reign of tyrants and liars, there have arisen men to free us. Where do these men come from?

Usually from the deserts, from the solitude of waste places. Deserts of sand and rock, like David and Amos, like Mohammed, the camel driver of Arabia. Deserts of obscurity, like Shake-speare. Deserts of blackness, like Milton.

It is at dusk of an April evening that we can best hear the "pipes of Pan," the sweet music which fills us with longing for the lost Eden.

Sometimes it is as the songs of birds, sometimes as the wind in the little branches, sometimes as the lap of ice-freed waters. The music is elusive, half-heard, and is not for the ears of the worldly wise or the cynic.

When God confiscated Eden he did not leave us without com-fort. He sent us Gabriel for a messenger, Michael to draw his sword in our defence against the lies of Beelzebub, Azrael to administer sweet death which is once only; and Pan.

The Great God Pan, the ancients called him. But they were wrong. Pan is not God. If a modern Aesop were to tell the fable, it might go like this:

"Do not array me in bright robes, do not give me the glorious wings of an angel. Clothe me, rather, as a faun; give me the active legs and cloven hooves of a goat, that I may more easily leap through the grass and the shrubbery and elude capture; lest, perhaps, these mortals will seek to confine me, bow the knee to me, garland me, and beatify me.

"And, lest I fall into temptation, as Satan did, give me a reminder of that accursed one to keep me humble. Give me bat's ears and curved horns."

And the Lord God saw that it was good to do so. And Pan will not allow himself to be worshipped, for worship is for the Lord God alone.

And to this day you cannot catch Pan to confine him, to put him on an altar. For Pan is fleet of foot and very agile, and when we wish to gaze on him he leaps between the tree boles, and we rub our eyes and say: "It was a moose, or a deer!" And he becomes one with the shades of dusk and the lap of waters.

Pan is for the comfort of beasts, since man turned against them his shards and flints, and forgot that they were related to him in the vale of Eden—which he lost in his heart. But our feet remain on the verdure, among the flowers, deep in the cool moss.

Pan is God's servant to unveil the world of nature, as Azrael is the guide to lead us through the curtains of our finite prison to the eternal dimension where there is neither time nor place, where there is neither weeping nor sorrow, where all things are made new and the wards of Pan may lie down in peace together.

No. Pan is not God; not to be worshipped.

He is only the doorman of the Word which went forth from the void. The impresario of the Song of Seven Days.

Hark! Do you not hear his pipes in the dry reeds, summoning the sheathed legions to burgeon anew?

The New Heaven and the New Earth are here and now! Not in the minds of the sophisticated, not in the test tubes and retorts, but where they have always been—in the hearts of men of good will!

Gloria in Excelsis!

CHAPTER XIV

Reflections

The Golden Ages of the past were golden not because there was no misery, no hunger, no mutilation, no tragedy. There were all these.

They were golden because the spirit of man looked upward to Infinity, not downward to the clay of his feet. They were golden because the physical and spiritual had not been divided, separated, dissected as a biologist dissects a toad so that it becomes mere pieces—things of no value.

In misery a man had the comfort of his Gods.

In hunger a man found satisfaction in contemplation.

In mutilation proud acceptance could say: "See the empty socket! Seat of the eye I left on the Oxus!" or:

> "Strip his sleeve and show his scars and say,
> These wounds had I upon Saint Crispin's day."

In war was music and high purpose. *Ha-ha!* snorted the pan-oplied war horse, all among the trumpets and the smoke and the shoutings. Blows were not crafty, nor death craven.

Tragedy raised the soul to greater heights than security could ever do.

And the world was still mystery.

The "known world" of the Greeks and Romans is to be spied out by way of the old maps in the back of the atlas. We can peer at the bulk of trans-Caucasian Russia and see a great blank marked "Scythia." The word itself is an adventure in imagination. So is "Bessarabia," that barbarous land of fierce Sarmatians, scene of Ovid's exile! Our pulses quicken at the thought of the great bears and wild horsemen of the steppes.

For Africa there is only a narrow strip of the Mediterranean coast, bleeding off into another blank called the "Libyan Desert," beyond which were apes and ivory . . .

There was no America.

No Australia.

But somewhere in the dim West, so they said, lay the Lost City of Atlantis.

Romance; adventure; these aroused emotion and bred sentiment. These were the stuff of dreams.

Now we have tasted too much of the world, and the bile is in our mouths. We have conquered not men only, but oceans, continents, mountains, deserts of sand, and deserts of everlasting snow.

We have died—not always heroically, but too often anonymously, corruptly, bestially; in heaps, in droves, in helpless flocks of men and women, babes and ancients.

And now, sickened, we look again at the clay of our feet.

But much more remains than we think.

There are other realms, other courts, other worlds within our world. Romance and adventure are not dead.

If the realms of one challenge have been overrun; if the cities have been sacked and ground to dust, as Josiah ground the idols of old; if we have burnt with fire the courts of the continents; if we have trampled through their broken colonnades and under their roofless temples; if we have measured, surveyed, counted, added up, subtracted from, and written down the earth and the fullness thereof in our ledger books; if we have reduced her to numbers, graphs, and formulas for the maws of automation— that is not all. Hope still lies within Pandora's Box. The earth is still our mother and our teacher—unfathomable, mysterious, and ever-renewing.

The Spirit of God is still our Father, ever pardoning, ever inspiring. There remains still the scented wind to bring to us the Aeolian sweetness of the white swan's throat.

There remains still the soil, the dust of our nativity and our birthright. What it can do for us can best be told by the pen of Eiluned Lewis:

> We who are born
> In country places,
> Far from cities
> And shifting faces,
> We have a birthright
> No man can sell,
> And a secret joy
> No man can tell.

We can still walk behind the plough, even though we have no plough tail of our own.

In the clear-cut furrow—our feet in the damp earth, the good smell of loam lingering on the wine-sweet air of morning—we can see (for now we enter the world of imagination, which is closest to the heart of reality), we can see, I say, the milk-white oxen straining at the yoke chain, while the hum of the tractor is but the beast's outblown and scented breath.

Slowly, steadily they plod, while Cicero at our side exclaims: "Surely, there is nothing better than farming, nothing more fruitful, nothing more delightful, nothing more worthy of a free man."

Yes, now that we are numbered and known over the whole world—now that we carry identification to prove we live—the flavour, the piquancy of life appears to be gone.

All the more reason then to seek that grace without which we are mere numbers existing chronometrically, poor marionettes subject to the pull of strings held by the new dictators of technological fashion and taste.

And there is still the North.

Canada is a land of twenty million people, squashed into a narrow band of security and standard of living which lies smeared along her southern border.

She is a land of mountains and forests and far tundras, where men could find themselves, express themselves, and be masters of their lives.

Twenty million people who say the old days, the old ways, are no more; who say we must adapt ourselves to a new, circumscribed world; while a great unknown world lies at our doorstep!

Before we in Canada talk so glibly of the benefits we can offer emerging nations, let us cure ourselves of our own green sickness and emerge into our own land.

A new age of discovery is before us, but senses are dulled and our imaginations overlaid. We dream of a grandeur which we do not possess. We wear a cloak we have not paid for.

Before we know where we can go, we must look back whence we came. We must cease to disallow and denigrate the past. We must rediscover the good society, and direct ourselves towards that rather than towards mere affluence.

First of all by humility, by ceasing to behave like a lot of spoilt "gimme" kids or peevish godlings. We will only cease to regard the world as a toy to be torn to pieces—"our oyster," to use a popular expression—when we recognise the difference between knowledge and wisdom. The real problems of our society cannot be resolved by more plenty, when already it is surfeited, and we must substitute good values as a yardstick by which to measure our material wealth and possessions. And by this yardstick we may find we are poor indeed. This new approach will really be a step forward rather than backward, for the past is the blueprint of the future, and anyone who thinks he can find the road ahead without reference to the way we came by, deceives himself.

The countryman, better than anyone, knows that in travelling towards an unknown country he must continually pause and look back to get his bearings and keep his direction. He profits by everything he has seen, heard, and felt on the back trail. He will instantly recognise danger spots by eye and ear, and will not be so foolish as to walk into a swamp, attempt to swim a rapid, or become lost in deep and thorny thickets.

He will recognise nourishing from poisonous berries; he will know where water is before he comes to it. He will, above all, be alerted from within by those instinctual promptings which have been sharpened by use and experience.

Only by looking back and seeing the farm table with its oven-new bread, its cream, its fresh unfrozen fruits and vegetables, its home-cured meats and golden butter; only by resavouring in our minds the nourishing goodness of these things can we realise how uniformly bad is most of the food we eat today. The flavour-less, sour metallic stews; the refrigerated, desiccated, manipulated fruits and vegetables; the dehydrated, irradiated, homogenized cereals and honey; the frozen, pressed, processed meats, juiceless and chemical-tainted. It comes as a shock to realise that not only the ingredients but the actual cooking is bad. If you have ever stopped by a roadside café in France; if you have been served in a jiffy with an *omelette aux herbes, petit-pois,* and a bottle of red wine; if you have eaten bread with the very poor, or fruits with primitive people, you will understand this.

And our minds have received the same treatment. These too have been served in a hurry with packaged foods—sterile, taste-less, dull—which can only be ingested when slopped over with red sauce.

Dull arithmetic books with figures of ill-conceived and robot-like caricatures of elves and gnomes. Horrible travesties of na-ture's lovely animals twisted and contorted, made funny and vul-gar, under the undignified names of Bugs Bunny and Mickey Mouse! These are a far cry from what we see when we look back to the old books of natural history—to Seton Thompson or *The Jungle Books* or *The Wind in the Willows.*

So it is time for twenty million people to stop being absorbed with do-gooding, sex, status symbols, and "a share of our national wealth," and think about what can be done to build a free, self-reliant nation, and halt its imminent decay by manning the thin red line of civilisation.

Why did so many people leave the countryside?
We lost our heads. We lost the habits of caution and thrift.

We had to have the good things of which we had been too long deprived. We could pay later. But alas! How soon are these good things outdated. We had reached that state envisaged by Wilde in the words: "A generation that knows the price of everything and the value of nothing."

Once I helped such a couple pack up and leave.

"What about the organ and them books?" said the farmer.

"Oh, we don't want that old junk in the city—just leave it."

The farmer looked away. I saw him take his hard red hands from his pockets and look at them curiously, then stare out of the window. Was he seeing his mother sitting at the old harmonium playing the evening hymn? Was he hearing her read about little Nell and her grandfather from the dusty red book which lay on the floor with a Bible, a Shakespeare, and a book or two of verse? I don't know. He said: "O.K. I guess we're loaded."

A neighbour bought the farm to add field on field. The house was used for storing grain, and the mice made nests inside the old organ with the paper from the books. The farmer got a job in town—perhaps as a janitor, perhaps working on the city garbage crew or in a machine shop. In the evening, in the beer parlour, he met others like himself—landless labourers—and they would tell fellows like me what had happened. They shook their heads over their beer and said: "I guess times have changed" and: "You can't stop progress."

And sometimes the wives, caught off guard, would forget, and say: "The farm was surely nice. You know, I used to milk cows—we had one called Beauty—but there! There's no future in farming, and you have to be *practical*."

And here the words of Peter Howard, ex-Fleet Street journalist, now a working farmer, are applicable. He wrote about "that long-term exercise of brain and muscle and humility which is the education the soil offers to all who serve it with hands and hearts." And again: "To be at grips with the earth, to bleed and sweat and be bruised in the battle with it, is an age-old exercise which educates men and leaves them different. Their sense of values is renewed. They have something unshakable in the heart of them." To which Father Chapdelaine of *Maria Chapdelaine,* an epic of pioneer life in Quebec, would say "Amen."

That unshakability is at variance with the manipulators of technocracy, but I believe that there are Canadian men and women, youths and girls, who will dare to achieve it, although it may mean battling against governments, against technocrats, against the merchants of standard of living, against central selling agencies and unions, against society itself.

A nation of people—human, warmhearted, understanding, accepting—is worth more than any number of power dams or efficiently run industrial and commercial enterprises; more than any amount of Mercy, Justice, and Virtue institutionalized under the dead hand of dehumanized uniformity or orthodoxy.

To gain the whole world at the risk of losing our souls appears to be the object of today's society.

There is a residue of rural life and manners left. It is disappearing fast, and may die with this generation. Already it is apologised for, but a trace still colours the life of Silton Village and the Rural Municipality. We have the Reeve, an office that goes back certainly to Saxon times, and is probably pre-Roman. Within the Council rests the last vestige of the tradition that farmers can manage their own affairs. If we change to the proposed Counties that will be lost.

The village itself retains the ancient pattern, even if few recognise it as significant of God, man, earth. The Church is central and overlooking, like the eye of God. The cottages and houses are grouped around it, symbols of man's occupancy. The fields unfold all around, spreading out their pattern of brown, gold, green, and yellow, yielding their mysterious substances as they are splashed by rain or caressed by sun, sleeping in winter beneath the kindly snows which insure their inviolate rest. By the main street stands the village pump, and near to it is the Village Hall of the church teas and fowl suppers. There are still farmers who are more weather-wise than the official broadcast weather reports, men who know how to sow when the moon is waxing and to geld when she wanes. Let the experts say what they like, these men have seen their springs and wells rise and fall with the movements of the Queen of Night. And there are those who know how to "witch" for water. Our Silton well was found that way, and the "witcher" is here today. He is our storekeeper. There are still men who can physic a sick animal, whose ready hands still hold the ancient shepherd's craft when a new calf or a litter of piglets must leave the warmth of the womb; and they know, too, how to allay the fears of the sick mothers. There are those who do not kill their bees, who know the many thousands of years of relationship between us and the swarms of the golden hive; who know how to tap on the skip and announce a marriage or a death; you must "tell the bees" if you want them to thrive. These things are still spoken and pondered among those who gather at George's garage, which might have been a smithy.

There is still that service we call "yeoman" for a very good reason; the services which does not ask for pay, but goes at once with willing hands whenever there is sickness, sorrow, or work beyond one man's doing; that feeds the beast astray first, and lets the owner know its whereabouts second; that stops instantly on the road for a foot traveller or for tire or engine trouble.

But there are no shepherds. Only the bishops carry the crook, the long arm of God, the crook that nestled so easily to the hand of David, of Amos, of old Iden and the South Saxons of my youth on the downlands of Sussex and the salt marshes of Kent.

Once the shepherd was buried with a lock of wool in his hand. It was his passport to show to St. Peter. It explained his absence from Sunday Mass; it identified him as one who had heard his Saviour's voice in another great cathedral of arching skies and mint-sweet pastures, where the little birds nested and the lark lifted his heart to Heaven's gate. The faithful shepherd does not leave his sheep.

Out West on the High Plains there are lonely men who also

stay with their bands of woolly ewes. (They do not say flocks.) But these are called sheep herders, and are despised. Just before Christmas we heard a radio man interview one, but he was a young city man who knew nothing about crafts, and he did not ask the questions which would have unfolded this shepherd's love of nature, his knowledge of weather and flowers and wild things; nor his intimate knowledge of anatomy, sickness, and cures; nor the hundred and one other things that make a shepherd dedicated and happy out alone on the brittle short-grass prairie. From the interview one would think only that here was a silly old man who, like Grandpa, didn't know enough not to waste his life.

That is why in New Mexico the sheep are left to the care of the status-less Mexicans. At night after a day's shearing the *cocinero* makes coffee, and the shepherd folk sit in a close circle and sing to a softly plucked guitar while the desert air blows cool over the backs of the folded flocks, and the desert moon swings low as if eager to hear the shepherd music that once piped from the hills of Bethlehem.

You cannot think of sheep apart from God. Perhaps that is why we rationalistic and materialistic people leave the tending of them to lowly folk like Basques and Mexicans and Navajos. We hate the *baa*-ing of the cropping flock. It pricks our conscience.

And there are the arts of housewifery. The making of cordials, wine from wild fruits and from rhubarb and from humble dandelions, whose gold is witchery; and then the kitchen becomes the still room. And there is tea of yarrow, and goose grease saved against the winter's cold, and patchwork quilting. There is a lady who weaves mats from baling twine in a pattern as old as Chaucer's hand of writ.

Today Hope made bread. When she had lifted it from the oven she called out, as she always does: "Come and smell it!" There they lay, the loaves, belly up. She raised the snowy cloth, and

I bowed my head to the smell, with tight-shut eyes. Yet I saw not darkness but light, the light of the sun which had browned the hard grains, as the oven had browned the crusty loaves. I heard the tug of the plough as it turned the furrow slice—do we not say a slice of bread? I heard the screech of the seed drill and the patter of the rain; the rustle of the blades like the froufrou of silk as they shot upwards, pausing neither night nor day, growing while the farmer slept. And the loaves talked too; quietly, for the ears of understanding: "Speed the plough, speed the plough. Man must be fed—speed the plough." And I heard a still small voice from the days of our long-buried past, and the voice said: "Not as our fathers did eat manna in the desert . . . but the bread of everlasting life." And I opened my eyes, and Hope turned a loaf upward to show the cross she had slashed in the dough with her big knife. And we smiled at each other across the table.

We long ago achieved the sufficiency we prayed for. But we forgot many things, when we found we could hoard and store and increase. To grow wheat for man's bread was not enough. The King and the peasant were divided by the middlemen, the merchants, the speculators, who made money an end instead of a means. It became a faith. And the new faith begins to cover the earth. Its high priests find the smell of the most deadly sprays infinitely sweeter than the free-flung scent of the flowers they must blacken and wither. The hum of the low-flying planes must silence the ancient song of the grasshoppers, put here to enforce the law of fat years and lean, lest we waste and glutton and waste again.

The stink of commerce, like an evil cloud, crosses the oceans of the world. It fills the river valleys, it seeps into every barranca, every kloof, every canyon and wadi and gulch, rising and spreading over the uplands of Chemisa and Karoo, and across the hot plains of Spinifex. It lies thick among the jungle trees; and in the hearts of the mountains. It covers the ice caps of north and south. This is that same stink which reduced the half-breeds and Indians to beggary, which caught up with the Boers of the Transvaal. It will destroy many more peoples and cultures, from the flat-faced herdsmen of the Gobi to the naked, simple people of the Amazon rain forest.

Few have escaped, even now.

Here, perhaps, a *vaquero* boils his coffee among the dotted mesquite; there a Masai girl feeds with dung a cooking fire; or a Xhosa woman pushes together the thorns which crackle under her pot, the blue smoke pluming upward like the signal of a lost cause.

And when night falls the tiny pinpoints of flame, flickering in the velvet black, may be the last sanctuary lamp of the last Hearth-Altars of man. They speak to the trembling stars above— like calling to like. They tell in little squeaks and soft puffs and tiny crackles of the folly of man, who was born into beauty and saw it not.

We cannot change things. We cannot go back. But we could try to retain enough of the spirit to go forward taking our hearth-altars with us, so that the past and the future may come to terms. There is still a wealth of understanding and of commonsense. The story which I was thinking of in May is still there to rediscover. If we put off sophistry, if we become like children, if we turn to the source of life. There is only the way of the Spirit—no other way on earth . . .

It may be that Black Africa will yet retain a little of what we lost when we chose a stink for a sweet savour; when we turned from the daughter of Zion to embrace Mammon and pollute the earth. It may yet be Africa's destiny to show us the Way.

Christians, Jews, and others who worship God should never be heard to grumble, for have they not great words to ponder on? "How goodly are thy tents, O Jacob, and thy tabernacles, O Israel."

Many have come since Balaam to curse; many have remained to bless.

The time has come to choose whether we shall live by the push button or by the arts of man. This will mean, among other things, that the city must re-evaluate the things of rural life in terms of civilisation.

I record here a quotation from an article in a Canadian rural paper, which is headed: "The 'Turmoil of Change' Hits Rural Youth." It says:

> *Everyone is talking about "the turmoil of change." Few people are untouched by it.*
>
> *Here are examples of the things being said:*
>
> Farm Forum Guide, *January 4: "Rural communities have higher school dropout rates and lower college graduation rates . . . It is easy for a farm boy to use the excuse that he 'likes to work with his hands' . . .*
>
> *"Compared with urban areas, all provinces in Eastern Canada are failing to train their farm young people to fit into the rapidly changing economic environment of today, says a recent study."*
>
> Ina Burns, *in* The Family Herald: *"The farm boy finds himself swept into 4-H work which further prepares him for a life that will almost certainly be denied him . . .*
>
> *"No one would want to teach youngsters a dislike for country living, but we can help them discover something of worth beyond the south forty, to become more flexible, to serve humanity in other ways than by food production. We can teach them that a farm background in these days is no longer a farm boy's birthright, can be an important springboard to success if they know how to leap from it.*
>
> *"One cannot deny that 4-H has contributed a great deal— [but] does 4-H keep up with progress?*
>
> *"Most projects are time-honored: beef and dairy calves, swine and tractor clubs. There are new types of projects, but in only two provinces, Manitoba and Saskatchewan, have 4-H Career Guidance Clubs been organized."*

So speaks the sausage machine. This is the voice of commercialism. "Liking to work with his hands" need not be an excuse, but a real affirmation of preference. A farm *may* be a boy's birthright. Canada has thousands of unoccupied acres. It need not be denied him. I know of no great, happy, or ultimately successful man whose greatness, happiness, or success resulted from "career guidance!" The countryman is buried before he is dead.

My other quotation is a letter to *The Field*, a British country magazine, by a retired working man. Again I quote:

> *Sir, — I was thinking about the great increase in crime and vandalism as compared to when I was a "teenager." Then the crimes were always blamed on poverty by all social reformers. Their arguments were that if the unemployment problem was solved crime would cease.*
>
> *But now that "the people never had it so good" and the standard of living is improving all the time, instead of Utopia there is terrible vandalism and crimes increase every week.*
>
> *Comparing life today to when I was a lad, the great difference is that today there are no facilities for working chaps and lads to keep a few poultry, a flight of pigeons, pigs or even rabbits.*
>
> *In some cases the tin-pot Caesars on the local council refuse people the right to keep dogs, so what is a chap to do with his leisure? Bingo, bowling alleys, drink, horror films at the local cinemas?*
>
> *When I remember the loving care working lads used to lavish on their pigeons, their whippets, their hens, their ducks, and in a few cases their small-holdings, all of which helped to make the St. Vitus dance of the conveyor-belts endurable, then I think I have found the cause of the present-day unrest.*
>
> *But the hundreds of happy little hen-pens that I remember as a lad are now all gone, buried under slabs of concrete and brick boxes, the graveyard of the working chap's hopes and visions of what God created him for. That is why people feel that life now is so aimless.*
>
> Eric Ashton
>
> *Hyde, Cheshire*

There is a case to be made for country hobbies even in an urban setting which will strike a note familiar to many. We think of our canaries, rabbits, pigeons, poultry, budgerigars, bantams; our gardens; our roses—Maréchal Niel, Madame Melba, Gloire de Dijon; our bulbs—narcissi, hyacinths, daffodils; our pergolas, our trellises, our pathways, all built or made, like our hutches, our cages, our chickenhouses, by ourselves—not bought ready-made.

If the great landowners evolved the famous breeds of cattle, horses, and sheep, it was the working men of England who bred the smaller birds, the whippets, the ferrets, and the world-renowned types of poultry—men like Tom Barron, who improved the Leghorns.

It was the spare-time hobbyists of Britain who gave us new vegetables.

How did we learn all this? How were we able at an early age to distinguish a speckled Sussex hen from a silver-spangled Hamburg? A Norwich from a Yorkshire canary? A Nun from a Pouter, or a Tumbler from a Homing pigeon? How many grade-twelve students know what a savoy cabbage is like? Or the difference between a summer turnip and a swede?

We learnt all this from our books, our boys' magazines; books on poultry, cage birds, gardening, and goat keeping. I had *Saturday in My Garden* to show me how to separate tubers from corms and bulbs, how to subsoil a patch of ground for celery, how to prune the apple trees and rose bushes.

This was what kept a boy in the outdoors in rain and shine. This was what built bone and muscle. This was what inculcated that sense of responsibility. This was adventure. We all want to possess something of our own—even a few barred-rock hens. And with ownership there is responsibility. How can this principle be applied today in our society? How can the city boy or girl fulfill this longing for a patch of ground, a hutch of rabbits? Something to take them out of themselves and put their brains to work in tune with nature, so as to come into contact with the soil at an early age—willingly, not by direction.

So-called nature-study groups do not accomplish this. Neither do hikes and lectures. These are too much of the classroom. The

approach is too directed, too pseudo-scientific. Classroom study
of agriculture does not inculcate love for the soil, for again it
is too much engrossed with the technical study of machinery and
fertilizers, too biological in its presentation of plant and animal
growth. The imagination is not excited. Far better that schools
encourage the reading of books on rural life and natural history.
A really good magazine on back-yard activities could do wonders.
I have searched our libraries and bookstores in vain for the kind
of books we had.

But by far the best school is experience, and to gain this we
must give the young people a chance to milk a cow or dig some
potatoes, or at least have a setting hen and some eggs to care
for. Then the youngster will find everything out for himself, by
himself, not as one of a group. There is land enough! An allot-
ment area close by any city would be worth many public parks
and playgrounds—desirable though these may be—because in a
park a man cannot dig up a bit of ground for cabbages, a girl
cannot call a tree hers, and a boy would not be allowed to keep
a pen of bantams.

Now that we are so affluent, let us reassess the road ahead by
finding the old landmarks, those that have not been completely
abolished. We must turn again to redig the blown-in, sand-filled
wells of our fathers. Recapture the riches of thought and speech
and verse. Redignify ourselves. Wash off the dust of the market-
place, reclothe ourselves in the robes of high purpose. Rediscover
the beauty of holiness and wisdom—that wisdom, that holiness
which flutters within a kiss between lovers, within the arms of a
mother cradling her first-born and pondering the mystery in her
heart. The wisdom and holiness which tells us that Paradise (if
we choose it) begins with our first breath, Heaven with our last.

This shall be the key to open up the real world we must look
to if we are to remain human.

The fields have been somewhat ploughed before, but the husbandman who dressed them preferred the fleshpots, and let them
lie. Some faint, overgrassed furrows still show the way to their
cultivation.

These are fields of understanding. The fallow fields of compassion and grace. The fields which ask our sweat, our labour, our love.

Neither brass nor iron will suffice to loosen the stubborn, neglected sod, and we shall call on no Tubal-Cain, for the steel share is too brittle, too unyielding, and the sword will break off at the hilt. Nor shall the edged scalpel of the scientist prevail; it would merely dull its blade before ever it discovered the jewel in the toad's head.

Sweat and tears and joy; sunshine, rain, and the season, will join with our clever hands to accomplish the heart's desire.

Gently is the way to win.

It is in the sweat of these fields that we shall exchange status for stature, in which we shall find release from peering into what is beyond our finite minds. If it troubles us that we see but darkly, as through a glass, yet let us remember that, left to vain reasoning, we shall inevitably die, like C. S. Lewis's bee, upon the window-sill.

Only with our feet on the beating heart of the earth can we reach up to touch with a finger the soft, translucent sky.

Only then shall we know that man is not a creeping, peering thing, concerned with weaving his heartless metals into a thousand crafty shapes to shackle men's hearts and minds, to imprison their spirits within mathematical formulae.

Only then shall we cease to dig up men's bones and research into the lives of primitive man—which is mere guesswork at best.

Let us leave those withered bones to lie in peace, and turn rather to the indestructible, living words which past ages have left to us. Reach up and touch the sky!

And know that man, every man—the smallest, the meanest, the most ignorant—is spirit. That his life is God's gift—not a right. Man has no reward for man. Man cannot help man except in one way, by his acceptance of his humanity and the awareness of the indwelling spirit.

In no other way can we be free. Someday the rationalists, the

REFLECTIONS   **193**

experts, the atheists, and the manipulated will be gathered by
the hand of God and brought home. They are not less loved,
and those who come at the eleventh hour shall also have the
Vision Beautiful they now deny.

My hope is that somewhere in these pages, in which I have
contrasted the placid beauty of nature with the rat race of artificial life, there may be one single beam of that vision to bridge
the gulf.

One night last winter we heard Bill McNeil of the CBC inter-
viewing Sister Rebecca of the Sisterhood of Mary from Germany.
She said in her charming school English: "People of the open
nature are more able to understand the call. The call home to
the Lord, I mean. If we go the way of faith all would come by our
Heavenly Father. Then, guided by the Lord, we shall not want."

And I think this is an excellent place to write *finis* to a countryman's thoughts.

BIBLIOGRAPHY

Bell, Adrian, and Others	Articles in *The Countryman* (Bradbury, Agnew & Co., London)
Berton, Pierre	*The Comfortable Pew*, etc.
Caesar, Julius	*De Bello Gallico*
Carson, Rachel	*Silent Spring*
Chaucer, Geoffrey	*Canterbury Tales*
Chesterton, G. K.	*Selected Essays*
Cloete, Stewart	*Turning Wheels: The Great Trek of 1836*
Darwin, Charles	*On the Origin of Species by Means of Natural Selection*
Dixon-Scott, J.	*England under Trust*
Grzimek, B. and M.	*Serengeti Shall Not Die* (H. Hamilton, London, 1960)
Hémon, Louis	*Maria Chapdelaine*
Holland, Clive	*Thomas Hardy's Wessex Scene*
Homer	*The Odyssey*
Housman, A. E.	*A Shropshire Lad*
Huddleston, Rt. Rev. Trevor, Bishop of Masasi	*The True and Living God*
James, Henry	*Collected Works*
Javabu, Noni	*Drawn in Colour*
Langland, William	*The Vision of Piers Plowman*
Lewis, C. S.	*The Screwtape Letters*
	The Meaning of Pain
Marcus Aurelius	*Meditations*

Marshall, Catherine   *Beyond Ourselves* (McGraw-Hill, 1961)

Marx, Karl   *Das Kapital*

Massingham, H. J.   *The English Countryman* (1942)

Munnings, Sir Alfred   *An Artist's Life*

Neatby, Hilda   *So Little for the Mind*

Orwell, George   *1984*

Plato   *The Republic*

Pliny the Elder   *Natural History*

Priestley, J. B.   *Journey down a Rainbow*

Shevchenko, Tarus   *Poetical Works*

Sitwell, Sacheverell   *Splendours and Miseries*

Swift, Jonathan   *Essays*

Thomas à Kempis   *Imitation of Christ*

Thompson, Seton   *Wild Animals I Have Known*

Thoreau, Henry   *A Journey down the Merimac and the Concord*

Trevelyan, G. M.   *A Social History of England* (Longman, Green, London and Toronto, 1942)

Van der Post, Laurens   *The Secret of the Kalahari*

Vogt, William   *The Road to Survival* (William Sloan, Inc., New York, 1948)

Walton, Isaac   *The Compleat Angler*

Watts, A.   *This Is It*

White, Gilbert   *The Natural History of Selbourne*

Whyte, William H., Jr.   *The Organization Man*

NOTES

CHAPTER I

1. Notwithstanding the above, the early settlers of the Silton district felt some uneasiness at the start of the troubles. They gathered at the big Charles Benjafield house (which still stands) and prepared to defend themselves from any roving Indians; but when, on the following day, one of their number "made it" to Regina to ask for arms, Lieutenant-Governor Dewdney sent back word that there was no danger. The settlers went home.

CHAPTER II

1. Man the nomad antedates, and may yet postdate, man the rooted citizen.

2. See *The Treaties Between Her Majesty Queen Victoria and the Indians of British North America, 1873–1900*. Reprinted by the Provincial Committee on Minority Groups, Saskatchewan, 1961.

CHAPTER III

1. The deadly danger of the various herbicides and pesticides was well brought out in Rachel Carson's *Silent Spring*. Since that book was published, the chemical industry (a multimillion-dollar one) has increased its advertising threefold. I have thousands of clippings from journals and newspapers all over the world dealing with what is a real peril to life and health, not only to wildlife but to man himself.

"The Season of the Ghastly Dew" is the headline for one editorial in the New York *Herald Tribune*. An article in the London *Field* states there is danger of complete infertility in many of the most spectacular and interesting wild birds of Europe.

The Nature Conservancy (England) points out (*Daily Mail*) that sea birds' eggs (long an article of food on the sea coast) are now badly contaminated. "It is clear," the article states, "that agricultural pesticides are contaminating the environment much more than anyone has suspected."

Yet the experts now say we cannot feed the world without their use! How shall we eventually live at all in a totally contaminated world? How did the world exist so long and supply food for man and beast?

CHAPTER IV

1. Weeds on summer-fallow land accomplish no such useful purpose as they do on waste or disturbed land. Instead they rob the land of moisture which is to be conserved for the following year.

2. Recently there has been a suggestion put out by at least one western university that farmers pay a share of the costs of research in agriculture—as if they had not always been doing so!

3. Hope's brother, Major John Onslow, who spent many years in Iraq and Jordan, tells me this is exactly as he has seen it done in those countries.

4. We lose even the authentic appearance of things which were only yesterday familiar to thousands. The illustrators of today's books and journals—usually underpaid young art students—do not investigate the very vehicles which can still be found in fence corners and sheds. I have some of these illustrations before me, showing wagons without poles, sleighs without bunks, buggies without eveners, harness without hames, and teams steered by clumsy individual lines lacking crosschecks. Cowboys of sixty years ago are shown in the habiliments of today's rodeo contestants; and saddles, snowshoes, axes, and so forth are horrible to behold. And much of this is what passes for *Canadiana*.

I have, by contrast, a copy of R. M. Ballantyne's *The Young Fur Traders* (written in 1856). This book once belonged to a school, but was thrown out and bought (by me) for ten cents at a secondhand store. Here is a really authentic story of a young man apprenticed to the Hudson's Bay Company in its heyday, a book which should be a must for young Canadians. But the illustrations are very special. Every detail of the trappers' and Indians' costumes is exact, and beautifully done in full-page water colour. Where can we find such books today?

People who remember the old *Strand* and *Wide World* magazines will remember the same kind of illustrations, done by real artists. Photographs are all very well, but you can't photograph Christopher Columbus or a cowboy long since dead.

Chapter V

1. According to Pliny the Younger and the old books, bears kept alive this way!

2. Northwestern Australia is commonly referred to as barren, dreary, and inhospitable. Yet my son, who lived there for some years on a cattle station, has told me something of the survival pattern of the Aborigines. They find a variety of roots; there are delicious desert melons (both food and drink), and there are succulent white grubs which he has himself extracted from the fallen gum trees and eaten.

3. According to a news item in an Alberta paper (March 1965) the University of Saskatchewan finds that children on entering high school have not the physique of former years, and attributes this to sedentary habits (including being driven to school) and to having few, if any, chores.

4. This was the site of Strathallan School, which was moved into Silton village, thus escaping a worse fate.

5. Charlotte Whitton (lately the Mayor of Ottawa) stated recently that 25 per cent of all Canadians are of *English* descent or birth.

Chapter VI

1. Catherine Marshall (*Beyond Ourselves*) has a good deal to say about the Lost Heritage in her first chapter. She refers to the "inner poverty" of youth caught up in today's age of materialism.

Chapter VII

1. The martyrdom of the peasant under the juggernaut of "progress" is so well indicated in *Piers Plowman* (William Langland, the fourteenth-century poet of rural Shropshire) in the words:

> . . . I was dreaming
> That Piers the plowman, painted bloodily
> Came in with a cross before the common people
> And like in all his limbs to our Lord Jesus.

Langland shows the real goodness of one to whom labour was sweet, and that only humble men like him could really save England and the world.

CHAPTER VIII

1. *The Farm and Ranch Review* of Calgary lately sent out questionnaires to farmers and others, and discovered that the coyote has more friends than has been supposed. More than 50 per cent of replies were in favour of the animal, as having a necessary place in the Great Plains environment.

2. See Sir Winston Churchill's "Jeremiah" speech to the British House of Commons on preparedness, about the time of World War II.

3. The playing about with "cowboy" guns is entirely at variance with correct military training, which teaches a proper regard for lethal weapons.

CHAPTER IX

1. This pastor, true to the peasant character so noticeable in French Canadian priests as well as in Protestant groups, thinks nothing of helping a disabled farmer by picking rocks, driving a tractor, or helping with the harvest.

2. This particular description applies really to the Arm River district, where I lived in early days. It is about sixty miles as the crow flies across the lake from Silton, but would not differ in general flavour from Red River to the Rockies.

3. This refers to some fifteen years ago, when gin was the height of fashion for young people. It was supposed, I believe, to have an aphrodisiac effect and "helped the party along." About this time Silton decided against public dances. One of the repercussions of the 1930's was that parents were indulgent in remembering what they didn't have.

CHAPTER XIII

1. "One generation passeth away and another generation cometh, but the earth abideth," says Ecclesiastes.

What kind of earth it shall be is for us to say. Shall it be torn, blasted, riven, fissured? Shall it be soaked in deadly poisons? Shall it be denuded of wildlife? Shall it be so manipulated by technology that the generation that cometh, doomed to frustration, shall curse the day it was born and, like Job, consider those twice happy that never were conceived in the womb?